T0143857

The Art of Jewish Living
The Shabbat Seder

A Teacher's Guide and Implementation Manual

by Dr. Ron Wolfson

A Project of The Federation of Jewish Mens Clubs and The University of Judaism

TABLE OF CONTENTS

THE ART OF JEWISH LIVING: THE SHABBAT SEDER—TEACHER'S MANUAL

Introduction

This Teacher's Manual and Implementation Guide for the *Art of Jewish Living: The Shabbat Seder* program of the Federation of Jewish Men's Clubs provides complete support for any group organizing and anyone teaching this course. Designed for the knowledgeable layperson who will teach the course, the Manual contains:

1) Teaching tips for presenting the content of the course
2) Detailed lesson plans for each session of the course
3) Additional background material on the Shabbat Seder
4) Implementation Guide for those responsible for organizing the *Art of Jewish Living* course in the local congregation or the educational setting

The Art of Jewish Living: The Shabbat Seder program has been developed as a vehicle for helping laypeople teach other laypeople the background and skills for "making Shabbes" in the home. The course can be taught in any adult education setting, be it formal programs, workshops or in home study by *havurot.* All one needs to teach the program is the textbook, the audiotape of the Hebrew blessings, the full complement of Shabbat Seder ritual items and this Teacher's Manual.

The teacher of the AJL course is the single most important factor in the successful implementation of this program. While it is true that some people might teach themselves how to do the Shabbat Seder with just the textbook, our experience has been that people learn to "make Shabbat" from *other people*, not from books and tapes. The decision to learn how to "make Shabbat" and then to introduce it into the home is a major step on the road to Jewish commitment. It has implications that reach well into the very fabric of family life. Your role as the leader in a program of this kind is much more than that of simply "teacher." You must be a "facilitator" and a "counselor," helping your students begin to create their own art of Jewish living.

FACILITATING THE ART OF JEWISH LIVING

A facilitator is one who helps someone become "facile" at something. Being facile means being at ease. Your goal as the facilitator of this course is to help the participants learn the Shabbat Seder well enough to be at ease with it. This is not an simple task. It will require your best communication skills. It will mandate an understanding attitude. It will demand that you understand the complicated process of leading another person to make significant changes in his/her religious behavior.

Remember, the *Art of Jewish Living* program is not a course which just teaches abstract material. Our goal is to change people's lives. We are asking people to learn a set of meanings and skills which we want them to implement in their homes *every week*! This is not like studying the history of the Jews in Spain. Ultimately, this course urges every participant to come home every Friday afternoon and prepare a formal meal and family celebration.

We are asking you to do much more than teach. Certainly, teaching is a major part of what you will do in this course. On the other hand, your best modeling and counseling skills will also be needed to achieve the goals of this program.

1) MODELING

"Modeling" refers to showing a behavior so others can imitate it. A "model" is someone who can serve as an artist's pattern. As a layperson who has learned to make Shabbat for yourself, you are a model for the aspiring "artists" in your class. They are far more apt to learn the "art" of Jewish living from someone who more closely resembles themselves than from a so-called "professional Jew." Having learned how to celebrate Shabbat yourself as a layperson, you can be a valuable example for them.

We have found that the "art" of Jewish living involves far more than simply learning the basic components of Jewish observance. In our interviews with lay families, we discovered that although most of them included the major elements of the Shabbat Seder in their celebration—candles, *Kiddush, hallah*—all of them had created an observance which was uniquely theirs. They did this by applying the basic strokes to their own composition of the Friday night ritual and then making them their own. Moreover, they told us that their own celebrations of the Shabbat Seder had indeed changed over the years. Sometimes in response to life-cycle stages, sometimes from the influence of new study or experiences, all these families *evolved* their own expression of Shabbat. Among the most important ways families learn to create a Shabbat experience is by adopting that which they have seen others do. Time after time, people told us that they learned to do one behavior or another from other people or families. As you will see in the profiles in the student text: The Goodglick family learned to bless their children from their friends the Silvermans. Karen Vinocur learned how to say *Kiddush* from her father. Elaine Albert learned how to celebrate the basic Shabbat rituals from a talented teacher. The real teaching you will do in this course will be modeling—demonstrating the behaviors and skills necessary to begin the process of creating Shabbat in the home.

You will notice in each lesson plan in the course, you will be demonstrating ritual behaviors. Every step you take will be important to the learners in your class. Even something as seemingly insignificant as which candle you light first or how you hold a *Kiddush* cup will be watched carefully. It is very important to remember that when people are learning a new skill, particularly one with religious significance, they want to get it right. Not just approximately right, but absolutely right. So, it will important for you to be an accurate model of all the behaviors you teach.

2) PRACTICE

After modeling, the next most important way to learn a new skill is to practice it. We all know that it is impossible to learn how to ride a bike by watching someone else ride a bike. Certainly, we can learn much by observation, but until we do it ourselves, we really cannot hope to learn how to do anything.

This is true with learning ritual behaviors as well. The participants in your class should be just that— *participants*. After they watch you demonstrate, they must participate. Most of the of time in your class will be devoted to the learners practicing the blessings and behaviors which make up the traditional Shabbat Seder. So, it is extremely important for you to understand how to set a climate for this participation.

First, *all practicing should be done as a group*. It would be extremely uncomfortable for people to take turns practicing alone in class. They are trying to learn material and behaviors which are very foreign to them. If they feel embarrassed, you are not likely to see them again. On the other hand, there is safety in numbers. They will know that the others in the class are also just learning. The combined voices of the group provide a safe environment to try out the foreign language or the new behavior. Rest assured, they will eventually pick it up. Let them practice as individuals at home.

Second, *your participation is critical* for the learners to learn. Modeling involves providing a pattern for them to follow. Therefore, at every step along the way, you participate with them. Your voice should be the loudest, especially at the beginning of the course. You should always participate in every run-through of a ritual behavior. The participants will feel so much more confident if they know that they can glance up at you and always see you doing the behavior as well.

Third, *provide time for practice*. Do not assume that the people have learned the words or the skill after one or two tries. It will take time for them really to become comfortable with these new behaviors. That is why every lesson begins with a *review* of all previously learned material. In this way, the participants will be able to practice what they have learned a number of times in class. This building upon previous practice is an extremely important key to the success of the program. Do not skip the review segments, even if you fall behind in the schedule.

3) COUNSELING

When people learn the skills to make Shabbat, they usually want to incorporate this celebration into their lives. If others in their immediate family take exception to this, there is the potential for conflict. That is when your role as counselor becomes extremely important.

The adoption of Jewish ritual practice in a family setting can be unsettling for spouses who are unwilling or unprepared to go along and for children who are not used to these new requirements. You may have participants in the class who are new converts to Judaism and have a whole variety of family concerns. There may be single parents in the group who face many difficulties in making Shabbat an important part of their family time. Other types can present their own unique requirements in the class: empty-nesters, singles, parents of teenagers, intermarried couples, and mixed marrieds, just to name a few.

You will not be expected to solve everyone of these people's problems, But, when you ask the participants to share their experiences as they begin to experiment with Shabbat at home, expect to hear a number of problems raised. Among the most common is: "What if my spouse doesn't go along with instituting a Shabbat Seder at home?"

This is a common stumbling block for many people. Ideally, a couple should attend the class together, learning together, and deciding together what they will introduce into their Friday night ceremony. But, often, one or another spouse will take the initiative and face the task of securing the cooperation of the other. Sometimes, the non-involved spouse will take a position of tolerance: "I don't buy it, but if it's important to you, go ahead." Sometimes, the non-involved spouse will refuse to allow it, absenting him/herself when Shabbat comes around. Sometimes the source of the objection is from negative memories of a rigid orthodoxy in a spouse's upbringing to which he/she rebelled. Sometimes it is a case on non-belief and a fear of feeling or being labeled a "hypocrite."

You will not be in a position to know if the source of this negativism comes from an objection to Jewish ritual or can be traced to other problems in their relationship, nor should you inquire. You will want to encourage the learner to engage the spouse in a constructive dialogue about the reasons for the objection. If the lines of communication can stay open, then the chances for resolving a situation of conflict are good.

Perhaps the most important part of your role as counselor is to offer support to the participant . You cannot hope to solve difficult problems in the time you have in the program. You can, however, be as supportive as possible, as encouraging as possible to the person. In extreme cases, you may want to offer to help the person get in touch with someone on the professional staff of the synagogue to help. Your Rabbi should certainly be able to help in cases of extreme conflict.

Another helpful move you can make is to encourage the participant to get the reluctant spouse or child to a Home Hospitality Shabbat experience. Often, when they see the beauty and meaning of Shabbat as lived in another home, the reluctant family member sees that other similar families have learned to adopt a Shabbat ritual as an important part of their family life.

I recall my own father's protestations about his "atheism." A devout reader of Spinoza, he clearly stated to his family his disbelief in God. On the other hand, he always participated in our weekly Shabbat table ritual. When I once asked him why, he responded that he did it because he knew it was important to my mother and he had come to value the precious family time it afforded him, a busy retail businessman. Whatever would happen the rest of the week, he knew that on Friday night, his family would be together, no matter what.

It will be important for you to share your personal experiences with unwilling family members, if any, and for you to encourage others in your class to share difficulties they may be having. Ultimately, the group itself can play an important role in giving the support necessary to those who must fight to institute a Shabbat ritual in their families.

4) TEACHING HEBREW

The teaching of the Hebrew blessings and prayers of the Shabbat Seder is an important goal of this program. You will have participants who have never learned to read Hebrew and you will have people who may be fluent Hebrew readers. Whatever the mix in your class, it is important to teach these Hebrew prayers.

You will notice in the textbook that every Hebrew blessing is presented in both the original Hebrew and transliteration. The transliteration code is found at the front of the learner's text. The layout of these texts allows the learner who can read Hebrew but does not understand it to follow in the two far right-hand columns—the Hebrew and English translation. Those learners who must read the Hebrew transliteration can use that column and the adjoining English translation column. We think you will find this layout to be quite useful in teaching the Hebrew.

You will also notice in the lesson plans for each session that detailed line-by-line instructions are given for the teaching of the Hebrew blessings. These instructions should help you in the translation of the Hebrew. We have tried to be as explicit as possible in these translations for we have found that adult learners are curious as to what each Hebrew word means. Even though the corresponding English translations sometimes seem a bit stilted, we feel it is important to give exact translations whenever possible.

The AJL program is not a course in Hebrew language. However, since the Hebrew prayers are so central to the Shabbat Seder, this emphasis on the Hebrew is important. Certainly, any participant can, and some will, opt not to learn the Hebrew, preferring the safety of the English. As you know, much is lost in the translation, including the mystery and beauty of using a language that has been part of Judaism for millenia. So, encourage your people at least to try to master the Hebrew, reminding them that it will become easier and easier with practice.

You will also note that the English translations of the Hebrew in the textbook session for the Shabbat Seder demonstration are sometimes different from those taught in the individual chapters on the specific blessings. We allow ourselves a more poetic translation in this part of the text, the part which will most likely become the text used at the Shabbat table itself.

5) SINGING

Singing is an important part of the Shabbat Seder. Although the blessings and prayers can certainly be recited in Hebrew or English, the chanting and singing of these same prayers adds so much beauty and fun to the experience that it is hard to imagine a Shabbat without it. On the other hand, you may find people in your class who cannot or will not sing.

Obviously, you cannot force people who don't like to sing to sing. But, you can point out that the quality of the voice is not an important ingredient in a successful Shabbat ritual. Encourage everyone in the class to learn the tunes for the blessings. Model this by singing all the tunes yourself, no matter what kind of voice you have.

Arrange to have a copy of the audiotape cassette of the Hebrew blessings for each participant. First, you should carefully listen to the tape provided with this Teacher's Manual to see if the tunes on the tape are the same as the tunes your congregation is used to singing. If there are major differences, contact your Cantor and ask him to record a tape of the tunes for the Hebrew blessings you intend to teach. Ask the Cantor not to use a "cantorial" voice. Rather, people just learning these chants need to follow a slow, deliberate rendition. Have copies of the tapes made at a local audio-visual store with high-speed tape duplication equipment.

The audiotapes can be an invaluable help to you in teaching the tunes for the blessings. Suggest to participants that they can listen and practice at leisure at home or even in the car. We know some learners who initially played the tape at the Shabbat dinner table so that all the family members could learn the tunes. In class, you will be helped to teach the tunes for the blessing by following these steps:

a) PRACTICE the Hebrew words FIRST. Much of the lesson will be devoted to translating and practicing the pronunciations of the Hebrew words. It is hard to learn to sing words that are unfamiliar, while the singing of the words themselves will help the participants learn the pronunciations.

b) TEACH the tunes LINE BY LINE. Begin with the first line. Sing the tune, slowly and clearly. Ask the learners to repeat the line after you while you sing along. Repeat the same line at least once and maybe twice. Then, go to the second line and repeat the same process. When you have learned the tune for the second line, go to the third line and repeat the same process. Then, return to the first line and sing the first, second and third lines together. Then, go on to the fourth line, and so on. The important thing to remember is not to go too far ahead without reviewing what you already have taught.

c) Some participants may come to the class knowing a tune for a part of the Seder which is different from the one you are teaching. A common example is someone who chants the candlelighting blessing using the tune for Hanukkah candles. On the one hand, they are singing the wrong "*nusah*" or melody. You may want gently to suggest that to them. On the other hand, if they already know a tune that has been used in their family from generation to generation, it may not be advisable to change their practice. You will need to play it by ear.

d) We have found that sheet music is not a big help in teaching the chanting of blessings. If people want sheet music, ask the Cantor to create some based on the tunes you use in the synagogue.

e) Remember to PRACTICE the chanting of the blessings at the beginning of each class in the Review section of the lesson.

6) ESTABLISHING SHABBAT HOME HOSPITALITY

One of the most interesting and successful parts of the AJL program is setting up home hospitality for the participants to experience a Shabbat dinner in another family's home. Ideally, the participant and his/her family will be invited to a host family on the Friday night immediately after the first session of the class. The participants will just have seen your demonstration of the complete traditional Shabbat Seder. Then, they will be exposed to a real family putting these rituals into practice.

The Committee on AJL should be able to identify a list of families who celebrate Shabbat willing to host learners. This list should be given to you before the first class session. On the list should be the host family's name, address, cross streets, phone number and names and ages of children. It should also list whether the family observes Kashrut or not.

This part of the program should have been listed on any publicity materials sent to the participants before they enroll in the class in order to alert them to save the first Friday night after the class begins for this purpose. If a family cannot take part in the home hospitality on the designated Friday night, you may be able to arrange for them to visit someone later in the course.

In the meantime, you will need to take a few minutes at the end of the first session to explain the program and to make matches of families.

During the introduction of the participants, make notes as to how many children and their ages in each person's family. You will also need to know if they live in the same approximate neighborhood as the host family. Try to match families that have similar age children and circumstances.

Prepare a 3 x 5 card with each host families name, children, address, cross streets and phone number on it to give to the learner who will be their guest. Suggest to the learners that they call the host family to introduce themselves over the phone and clarify directions and expected time of arrival. Suggest also to the learners that it would be proper Shabbat etiquette to send either flowers or wine to the hosts.

Ask the learners to pay careful attention to the Shabbat ritual as it is done in the host family. Tell them that each family will do the Shabbat Seder in a different way—some including much of what they saw in the demonstration; others less of the traditional ritual. Ask them to come to the next session prepared to share with the group what they experienced.

7) SCHEDULING THE CLASS

The *Art of Jewish Living: The Shabbat Seder* course can be taught in a time frame of between 9 and 12 contact hours of instruction. The scheduling of these hours will depend upon the structure of the adult education program in which the course is being offered. In the Implementation Guide found in the back of this Manual, three alternative schedules are suggested: 6 sessions of from 1 and 1/2 to 2 hours each (9-12 hours total), 8 sessions of 1 and 1/2 hours each (12 hours), and 10 sessions of 1 hour each (10 hours). Depending upon your timeframe, each session will cover different segments of the Shabbat Seder.

As the teacher of the course, you should be given some guidance as to what material to cover. Decisions about how much of the Hebrew to teach must be made, which version of the Birkat ha-Mazon will be taught, etc. You may even decide not to include some aspects of the traditional Shabbat Seder, again depending upon your objectives in teaching the course.

Although the material in the Teacher's Manual has been divided into 6 sessions, it is very simple to break the parts of the Seder out into whatever session framework you have to work with. The learner's text does not indicate sessions; one chapter is devoted to each of the ten steps in the traditional Shabbat Seder.

You should also feel free to expand or shorten your presentation and practice of various steps in the Shabbat Seder. For example, you may find that most of your participants know the hymn *Shalom Aleikhem* quite well, in which case you need not spend much time on it. As you go through the course, you will be able to tell which steps require more or less practice. Do not be concerned about adjusting your time schedule appropriately.

8) MONITORING ATTENDANCE

The *Art of Jewish Living: The Shabbat Seder* is not a long course. Each session is packed with information and practice. It is very important to emphasize that regular attendance is crucial for the success of the learner.

If your congregation establishes an AJL Campaign with a number of classes on the Shabbat Seder offered at different times on different days of the week, give participants a schedule of these classes. In case they do miss your class, they can then make up the session in someone else's class.

If a participant misses a class session, call the next day to follow up. Tell them you missed them in class and inquire about their health, or whatever the reason was for their absence. Tell them about the alternative class sessions. If you do not have more than one class, offer to help them make up the material later in the course. Remind them that since every new lesson begins with a review of previously learned material, they should be able to catch up rapidly. Ask them to cover the material they missed in the class by reading ahead in the textbook and listening to the tape. If you do not have the time to do this monitoring, ask someone else in the class to help you with this task.

Session 1 Outline

OVERVIEW:

In this lesson, (1) the course is introduced, (2) participants are given a chance to introduce themselves including the sharing of their own holiday memories, and (3) the instructor models the complete Shabbat Seder.

BACKGROUND:

Your task in this first session is to create a tone which will set the students' minds at ease—to assure them that Jewish observance can be taken on one step at a time, to give them confidence that they can, in fact, succeed in learning the blessings.

The key strategy in setting the appropriate climate in this first meeting is for you, the teacher, to be *inviting*. Pretend that you have invited these people into your own home, to share with them your own Shabbat observance. Just as you would treat a guest with understanding and patience, so here too these qualities should be evident as you begin to lead your charges into the adventure of learning and adopting the Shabbat experience. Like guests, the participants in your class will return home, free to adopt only that which they have found both meaningful and practical.

Your real role is modeling, enabling and advocating the Shabbat experience.

GOALS:

1. Participants will gain a clear understanding of the parameters of this course. This includes (1) that through this course they will master the *b'rakhot* and ritual actions involved in a traditional Shabbat Seder, and (2) they will attain the ability to shape and create their own family's Shabbat experience.

2. Participants will begin bonding into a class group through the sharing of personal insights and feelings.

3. Participants will observe the performance of a complete Friday night table service.

PREPARATION:

You will need to prepare a number of items to bring with you to each class session. For the first class, the list includes:

1) TEXT BOOKS. You will need one copy of *The Art of Jewish Living: The Shabbat Seder* by Dr. Ron Wolfson for each person enrolled in the class.

2) AUDIOTAPES. You will need one copy of the audiotape of the blessings in the Shabbat Seder for each participant.

3) SHABBAT SEDER ITEMS. You will need to bring the following things to set up the Shabbat Seder demonstration:

    a. *Tzedakah* Box
    b. Candlesticks
    c. Candles
    d. Matches
    e. *Kiddush* Cup(s)
    f. Wine (Israeli)
    g. *Hallah* bread (two unsliced loaves) and salt
    h. *Hallah* plate, cover and knife
    i. *Kipot* (head coverings)
    j. Shabbat Seder booklets (optional)
    k. White tablecloth
    l. Flowers
    m. One coin per person
    n. Washing laver, basin, towel and a source of water (a sink or pitcher)
    o. Cookies or "nosherei"

4) COFFEE. It is nice to arrange a coffee and tea set up for each class session.

5) TABLES. The best arrangement for your class will be long banquet tables around which everyone can sit comfortably. DO NOT USE student desks; they are usually too small for adults. You want to set up the room as if you were at the Shabbat table in your own home. Try to get comfortable chairs.

6) CHALKBOARD. You should have available a chalkboard and chalk or a flip chart with poster board and a marker with which to write.

7) NAME TAGS. Have name tags for each person in the group.

PROCEDURE:

PART ONE—INTRODUCTIONS

1. CLASS SET-UP

   Get to your assigned room at least 20 minutes before class is scheduled to begin. SET UP the tables and chairs banquet-style. ARRANGE the table for the Shabbat Seder demonstration, placing all the objects in their appropriate places. Place a small plastic or paper cup and a napkin at each participant's place. Fill the cup with some wine for *Kiddush*.

2. INTRODUCE yourself. Try to meet your class members in the hallway before class begins. Introduce yourself and welcome them into the room. This will set a warm tone for the class. When you are reasonably sure that those who have signed up have arrived, ask everyone to be seated. DISTRIBUTE name tags and ask the participants to fill-in their name. GIVE your name and the reason you are teaching this course. You might discuss your relationship to the Men's Clubs or the synagogue. For example, mention any leadership roles you fill. This should be brief.

3. PRESENT the course objectives. FIRST, tell the participants that this course is designed to present the complete traditional Friday night table ritual in all of its beauty. This will include a major focus on both the Hebrew and the English texts of the blessings. EMPHASIZE that even if they don't know how to read Hebrew, complete transliterations are in the text, and they will have an easy time learning to recite these blessings.

   SECOND, tell the participants that although the course will present a complete traditional Shabbat Seder, our goal is for each family to use these traditions as a starting point for evolving their own Shabbat experience.

   POINT OUT—we've called the course *The Art of Jewish Living*. Like an artist, each family should use tools and motifs to compose or design their own expression of Shabbat.

4. EMPHASIZE that participants are free to question anything and everything presented to them. But ASK them to maintain an open mind about the entire Shabbat Seder. Acknowledge that sometimes they may question whether they themselves would be comfortable doing a particular part of the Seder. Ask them not to do so, and to save their judgments about what they will include in their own observance until they have had the opportunity to learn it all.

PART TWO—STUDENT INTRODUCTIONS

1. ASK the students to introduce themselves by stating their name and the number and ages of their children, if any. Begin with the person seated to your right. (By the way, we recommend you sit at the table with the people which puts you on their level.) If a couple is attending together, be sure that each of them gives his/her own name.

2. RE-INTRODUCE yourself after everyone else has introduced themselves. Tell about your family.

PART THREE—HOLIDAY MEMORIES

1. TELL the participants that you want them to join with you in an exercise that will set the scene for our study of the Shabbat Seder.

2. SAY: "I want you to think back to any holiday celebration you can recall. It can be last week or ten years ago; it doesn't matter. If it can be memories of a Shabbat observance, so much the better. If you haven't had a Shabbat experience in a long time or if you've never had one, think of *any* holiday celebration you can remember." ALLOW the participants a few moments to begin thinking.

3. THEN SAY: "As you think about this experience, ask yourself the following questions:

   (1) Was it a special time in your life in some way?
   (2) What other people were involved?
   (3) Were there any ritual actions that you did?
   (4) Were any special objects used?
   (5) Did you eat anything?

   Try to think of one specific celebration that stands out in your mind."

   ASK if the directions need clarifying. SAY: "I will give you about one minute to call up the memory."

   AS TEACHER, GO FIRST. GIVE a personal example of your own holiday memory, i.e. "I remember Shabbes in my Grandmother's home. We called her Bobie. She would start Shabbat by going into the corner of the living room where she would light candles by herself. She would circle her hands over the flames and mumble some Hebrew words. No one else participated. She'd come out from underneath her hands and say 'Good Shabbes,' and that was it."

4. *(AN OPTION)* DIVIDE the group into pairs. Ask people to pair off to discuss their holiday memories with each other. SUGGEST that couples split off and discuss their memories with a new friend. ALLOW 3–4 minutes for the discussion. You should find that the discussions will be quite animated. If there is an odd number of participants, you sit with the odd-person out. If there is an even number, join one of the pairs and participate. This will send an important message to the group: that you intend to join with them in every aspect of the course, including those moments requiring personal disclosure.

5. RECONVENE the group. ASK for volunteers to share ONE aspect of their memory with the group. Be sure to limit their contributions to no more than 1 minute or you will lose the attention of the group. If you must cut someone off, assure them that there will be plenty of time throughout the course for additional reflection. The purpose of the exercise is to warm-up the group, not to give a soap box to one person. DO NOT FORCE people to contribute. ALL personal disclosure should be optional. If you wish, you can cue a person's memory with some of the questions you asked him/her to think about, i.e.: Do you remember using any special objects?"

6. MAKE THE POINT, which is, much of what goes on during holiday celebrations is what we call *"memory makers."* Whether your people remember Shabbat experiences or Passover Seders, EMPHASIZE to them that what they are going to learn in this course has the potential to create memories for their children, their family and guests, indeed for themselves.

PART FOUR—SHABBAT SEDER DEMONSTRATION

1. INTRODUCE the Shabbat Seder demonstration. TELL the participants that you are about to lead them through a demonstration of the entire Shabbat Seder. BEFORE you begin, however, REMIND them that your purpose is to introduce the entirety of the experience, fully realizing that each person will ultimately choose which of the parts of the Seder they feel comfortable with including in their personal observance.

   SHARE with them your understanding that much of the Hebrew may sound difficult, particularly if it is unfamiliar to the tongue. Some of the ritual actions may seem awkward. All of this is to be expected at first. ASSURE them that during the next weeks they will learn to master the Hebrew blessings and the ritual behaviors.

   SAY: "Starting with the very next class session, we will go back to the beginning of the Shabbat Seder and take each part, one step at a time, and practice it until we all feel comfortable with it. We are not in a hurry. YOU MAY WANT TO POINT OUT THE FOLLOWING: Some of you will be familiar with parts of the Seder; others will not. We have an excellent text to help us learn the procedures and the meaning behind them. We have an audiotape to help you learn the blessings."

   FINALLY, ADD THIS DISCLAIMER: "Do not be overwhelmed by what we are about to experience. You will also notice that the demonstration will take us about 40 minutes to complete. I want to assure you that in my home, the entire Shabbat ritual from candlelighting until the time we eat the meal lasts about 10–15 minutes. I promise you that once you learn the material and practice it a while, the entire experience will become easier and increasingly more fluent."

   It is extremely important to emphasize these points to your group. You will have many people to whom the traditional Shabbat Seder will seem to last an eternity and be entirely too difficult to master. We don't want to scare them off so they will need this reassurance.

2. MAKE THE POINT that *"The Art of Jewish Living"* series is based on an egalitarian approach to Jewish observance. Without going into detail, explain that while you will present the "traditional" roles played by men and women in the Shabbat Seder, modern sensibilities and situations may dictate a re-thinking of this matter. For example, you may want to foreshadow something they will learn in the next session—that, according to Jewish law, if a woman is not available to light Shabbat candles at the appointed time, a man is obligated to do so. POINT OUT that you will want the group to keep in mind traditional roles, but at the same time open their eyes to new possibilities. The important thing in the celebration is the *celebration*, not necessarily who does what.

3. BEGIN the Shabbat Seder by ASKING the participants to pretend that you are inviting them into your own home on a Friday night. Like any good guest, you want them to participate when you ask them to and to think of questions they may have about the actions you will ask them to do. However, for this session and this session only, you want them to keep their questions to themselves. In fact, you may suggest that they write down the questions that come to mind as you lead them through the Seder. ACKNOWLEDGE that this may be frustrating at first, but your purpose is to present the entirety of the Shabbat Seder uninterrupted so they can see the goal we are heading towards. They will, in fact, find it irresistible to ask questions, and you will judge which ones to answer and which to deflect, but you do want to set the tone of simulating the experience with as little interruption as possible.

4. DISTRIBUTE THE PARTICIPANT'S TEXTBOOKS. ASK THEM TO TURN TO THE CHAPTER ENTITLED "THE SHABBAT SEDER."

ASK what the word "seder" means. Most people will recognize it in association with Passover, the *Pesaḥ* Seder. ASK: "Does anyone know what it actually means?" Translate "seder" as "order." Just as the *Pesaḥ* celebration has an "order" to it, so too does the Shabbat table experience has a well-defined order. Point out that while the *Pesaḥ* Seder has a *Haggadah*, a prayer book which presents the order of the celebration, so too will we work with this chapter in the book which presents the complete Shabbat Seder.

5. OUTLINE the 10 parts of the Shabbat Seder. As you do, begin to teach the Hebrew terms for the actions to be taken. For example, SAY: "The first step in the Shabbat Seder is called "*Hakhanah L'Shabbat*," which means 'Preparation for Shabbat.' ASK the participants to repeat the Hebrew term. TELL them that you want them to become comfortable with the Hebrew terminology and the only way to do so is to practice using the Hebrew terms. Point out that some of the terms will be more familiar, such as "*ha-Motzi*." WRITE the transliterated Hebrew terms for each of the ten parts of the Shabbat Seder on the chalkboard or flip chart. Your list should look like this:

   1) *Hakhanah L'Shabbat*—Preparation for Shabbat
   2) *Hadlakat Nerot*—Candlelighting
   3) *Shalom Aleikhem*—"Peace be to you"
   4) *Birkot ha-Mishpaḥah*—Family Blessings
   5) *Kiddush*—Sanctification of the Day
   6) *Netilat Yadayim*—Washing the Hands
   7) *Ha-Motzi*—Blessing over Bread
   8) *Seudat Shabbat*—The Shabbat Meal
   9) *Z'mirot*—Shabbat Songs
   10) *Birkat ha-Mazon*—Grace after meals

ASK if there are any questions about the outline. This review of the outline will help the participants get an overview of the entire Shabbat Seder.

6. POINT to the layout of the Hebrew and transliterations in the text. EXPLAIN that those who cannot read Hebrew can follow along using the transliterations which are situated line-by-line next to the Hebrew texts. TELL the participants that starting with the next session, you will review the Hebrew word-by-word so they will know exactly what the blessings are saying.

7. TELL the students that you will be teaching them the tunes for the prayers which are most familiar to the majority of the congregation. Although you realize that some of them may know other tunes, for the purposes of the class, you will be using the synagogue tunes. Also, ASSURE them that those who are uncomfortable chanting the prayers are welcome simply to recite them. However, POINT OUT that music enhances the celebration and encourage them to try to sing along.

8. LEAD the participants through the entire Shabbat Seder demonstration. As you do, REINFORCE the names of the various parts of the Seder. They should follow the text in Chapter Two. ENCOURAGE them to join in when you recite the prayers and do the actions. If someone says "But we do this differently," ACKNOWLEDGE that there are many ways to do the parts of the Seder and you will discuss them during the coming weeks. Remind them that at this session you are asking them to pretend as if they were guests in your own home and you will be doing the ceremony as it is done there.

Here is a brief outline of what the demonstration should look like:

a) **Hakhanah L'Shabbat.**

   Briefly DISCUSS the process of preparing for Shabbat. GLOSS the work which must be done. POINT OUT the possiblity of assigning individual family members to each job.

   The demonstration BEGINS with *Tzedakah*. Actually PASS around the *tzedakah box* and ASK people to contribute a few coins.

   AN IDEA: since this is the first session of the course and some people may not have money with them, put a few pennies at each person's place so they will have something to put in the box. This will avoid embarrassing someone who does not have any change. The idea is for the people to feel the experience in a positive way and it would be a shame to start off with something they are unable to do.

   REMOVE the *tzedakah box* from the table when everyone has contributed the coins. Make sure everyone sees you do this, but don't tell them why, even if they ask. DEFLECT the question with "You'll find out next week!"

b) Hadlakat Nerot

ASK everyone to rise for *Hadlakat Nerot*. Strike a match, light the two candles, and blow out the match. Make sure the fire catches the wick totally so you don't end up with a burned out candle. TELL the group to watch you carefully and repeat what you do.

PLACE your hands over the flames, MOVE THEM, making a circle inward towards you three times. End up by COVERING your eyes with your hands. CHANT the blessing. Make sure you do not say "Amen" at the end of the blessing. When finished with the *b'rakhah*, hesitate a few seconds, uncover your eyes, look at the candles and then wish everyone "Shabbat Shalom." LEAVE your place and greet each participant with a kiss or handshake and a personal "Shabbat Shalom." The participants may be surprised by this, but they should catch on and begin to wish each other "Shabbat Shalom" in a similar way. It will "warm-up" the group as well as demonstrate that Shabbat is an opportunity for closeness.

There will probably be a number of questions at this point: "Do you have to circle your hands?" "Why don't we say 'Amen?'" etc. Try not to answer them now. Again, REMIND them that most questions will be answered at the next session or in the text.

c) Shalom Aleikhem.

INVITE the participants to sit down at their places. TURN to the *Shalom Aleikhem*. TELL them: "In our home, we like to join hands or put arms around shoulders and sway with the music. It makes singing much more fun. Please join me." GRAB the hands of your two neighbors and begin to sing. They should follow your lead and join in. SWAY with the music. Have fun with it. When you finish, SAY something like "That was great! You are good singers!"

d) Birkot ha-Mishpaḥah

INTRODUCE the next step by telling the participants that in this course we combine the traditional "*Eishet Ḥayil*" prayer for the wife with the blessings for the children, as well as some newer parallel prayers for the husband into one section called *Birkot ha-Mishpaḥah*—Family Blessings.

BEGIN with Blessings for the Children. PICK one female participant and pretend she is your child. ASK her to come to your place. STAND and PLACE your hands upon her head and RECITE "*Y'simeikh Elohim k'Sara, Rivka, Raḥel v'Leah.*"

Then, ASK a male participant to pretend he is your son and ask him to come to your place. STAND, PLACE your hands upon his head or on his shoulders and recite: "*Y'simkha Elohim k'Efrayim v'khi Menasheh.*"

Then, with one hand upon the head of each, RECITE the "Priestly Benediction" over both. Then, give each a kiss and whisper something personal, such as "I'm glad you're in this class" to each of them. Then, ask them to sit down.

CONTINUE with the *Eishet Ḥayil*. ASK all the men in the group to join in reciting the prayer in English. If there are couples in the group, suggest to the husband to kiss his wife after the prayer.

Then, ASK all the women to recite "Blessed is the Man" in English. Suggest to spouses to kiss after this as well.

By now, there will be some comment about "all the kissing." RESPOND with something like "Did you know that among married couples the average number of times they kiss daily is once!" ASSERT your position that kissing is good, especially on Shabbat.

e) Kiddush

OUTLINE the three parts of the Kiddush.

The **first paragraph** is from the Bible in the account of creation.

The **second part** is the blessing for wine.

The **third part** is the paragraph which actually sanctifies the Shabbat.

INVITE everyone to stand for the *Kiddush*. (You could choose to sit for *Kiddush*. There will be a detailed discussion of this option in the chapter on *Kiddush*. You should do what you do in your own home at this point.) BEGIN by asking everyone to raise his/her cup of wine. RECITE the "*Vayekhulu*" in English or Hebrew. Then CHANT the "*Borei p'ri ha-gafen*" and the third paragraph to the end. DO NOT sing "Amen" at the conclusion of the *Kiddush*. If the participants do, it is okay. Don't make a point of it now. DRINK the wine.

f) Netilat Yadayim

EXPLAIN that the Shabbat table is likened to the altar in the ancient Temple and as the priests of old, we symbolically wash our hands before breaking bread. OUTLINE the next procedure to them carefully. First, you will ask them to wash their hands in a particular way. You will show them how. Then, everyone will return to the table and recite the blessing for washing the hands together. TELL them not to talk between the time they wash until the moment they eat a piece of *ḥallah*, except for the recitation of the blessings. DO NOT tell them why there is no talking at this point. GO to the table set up for handwashing and DEMONSTRATE the proper procedure for washing.

FILL the washing cup with water from the sink tap or large pitcher. PLACE IT in your right hand. POUR some water over the left hand, wetting it from the wrist down. TAKE the cup in your left hand and repeat for your right hand. (Actually, the order of hands is arbitrary.) YOU MAY repeat the entire procedure twice more for a total of three times. If you are at a sink, it is good etiquette to refill the washing cup for the next person.

INVITE everyone else to follow your example. WALK back to the places at the table and give a signal to join in the blessing "*Al netilat yadayim.*"

g) Ha-Motzi

IMMEDIATELY UNCOVER the *ḥallot*. PLACE one *ḥallah* on top of the other, NICK the end of the top *ḥallah* with a knife, and then SIGNAL to everyone to join in the *ha-Motzi* blessing. TEAR or CUT off the end piece. SALT that piece. Then, place enough pieces of the "blessed" *ḥallah* on a plate and pass it around to everyone.

After you have eaten the first piece, SAY: "Now you can talk again. You probably have lots and lots of questions about what we just did. Try to save them for when we get there in the course. Or, of course, you can read ahead in the text."

h) Seudat Shabbat

DISTRIBUTE some cookies and *ḥallah* to the participants. If you have a coffee set-up, now would be the time for a coffee break. But, don't lose the momentum of the demonstration. TALK about the kind of meal you have at your home on Shabbat, how leisurely it is, and your favorite Shabbat foods. You might also welcome one or two questions from the group about what they just experienced. Limit this to only one or two. Again, remind them that all their questions will be answered beginning at the next session when you will begin all over again at the beginning in order to learn the "whys" and "hows" of each part of the Shabbat Seder.

i) Z'mirot

SING a few of the *Z'mirot* included in the Shabbat Seder chapter. Be sure to choose songs that most of the people will know, such as *Shabbat Shalom, Hiney ma tov u'mah na'im*, etc.

TELL the people that another important part of the meal/*Z'mirot* experience is to share feelings with each other. Suggest that one way to do this is to ask everyone at the table to share a response to "What was your favorite time this past week?" YOU begin with something short, such as "My favorite time last week was when I got to read a bed-time story to my kids." SHARE something that is meaningful to you. GO AROUND the table and ask everyone to share. If someone has trouble responding, allow him/her to pass.

j) Birkat ha-Mazon

TURN to the *Birkat ha-Mazon* in the Shabbat Seder chapter. INVITE the participants to follow along if they can as you lead the *Birkat ha-Mazon.*

BEGIN with "*Shir ha-Ma'alot.*" Chant it with whatever tune you will eventually teach. LEAD the "*Zimmun,*" the introduction to the *Birkat ha-Mazon.* SING the rest of the blessings in Hebrew. TELL the people that if they are unfamiliar with this, they will have the opportunity to learn the "short" version of the *Birkat ha-Mazon* by the end of the course. POINT OUT that the "long" version is included in the text in the Appendix.

When you have finished the *Birkat ha-Mazon*, point out that the entire Shabbat Seder demonstration took about 30–45 minutes because it was your first time through. REPEAT that the objective of the course is to enable the participants to become so familiar with each part of the Seder that, by the end of the course, the Shabbat Seder should only take 10–15 minutes up to the meal.

9. OUTLINE the "*Art of Jewish Living* Course."

Before class begins, you will have determined how many sessions there will be in the course. A number of models are listed in the IMPLEMENTATION GUIDE. DISTRIBUTE a copy of the course outline listing the dates of the sessions and which chapters you will deal with on those dates. GO OVER this outline with them.

10. ASSIGNMENTS

TELL the participants that their assignment for the next session is to read the text through the chapter on "*Hadlakat Nerot.*" RECOMMEND a selection of supplementary readings in the Appendix of the text. TELL them to BRING their candlesticks and two candles with them to the next session.

DISTRIBUTE the audiotapes of the Shabbat blessings. You will either have copied the audiotape provided with this Teacher's Manual or you may have re-recorded the tape using tunes familiar to your congregation. You should have enough tapes for every person in the course. ENCOURAGE the participants to listen to the tapes at home or while riding in the car. The more they can practice the Hebrew and the tunes, the easier it will be to integrate these blessings fully into their own Shabbat Seder observance.

11. SHABBAT HOME HOSPITALITY

If you have been able to arrange host families who will invite the participants to their home on the coming Shabbat or on the following one after, you will need to describe the arrangements for this part of the program. ENCOURAGE them to take advantage of this opportunity to see a real family celebrating Shabbat in their own home. Remind them that they will probably not see a Shabbat celebration exactly like the one they just experienced. That is part of the "art" of Jewish living—everyone takes the same basic strokes and composes their own picture of Shabbat. ASK those who will be guests in the home hospitality program to be prepared to share a few impressions of what they experience at the next class session.

SUGGEST to those who will be Shabbat guests that they should dress nicely and send wine or flowers to their hosts. ASK them not to compare what they saw in the demonstration at this session with what the host family does so as not to embarrass them.

12. SHABBAT OBSERVANCE AT HOME

If the participants are not visiting another family on the coming Shabbat, SUGGEST that they should begin their own observance of the Shabbat as soon as possible. They could begin with just the basics: *candlelighting, Kiddush, ha-Motzi* and a short *Birkat ha-Mazon.* ENCOURAGE them to experiment, to try things out. The most important thing they can do to prepare for the sessions is to try the steps of the Shabbat Seder in their own homes. REITERATE that at each session of the course, there will be the opportunity to share their concerns, failures and triumphs as they attempt to establish a Shabbat Seder observance in their families.

13. SEND-OFF

THANK each of the participants for coming to the course. TELL them you look forward to working with them in learning the Shabbat Seder. ASSURE them that the investment they are about to make in learning this material will be repaid to them over and over again with the hundreds of wonderful Shabbat evenings they will be able to have in the future. SAY: "I'll see you at the next session. Have a good week and 'Shabbat Shalom!'"

Session 2 Outline

OVERVIEW:

In this lesson, (1) the participants report on the Shabbat home visits or their own Shabbat experiences thus far, (2) learn about Shabbat preparation and (3) practice Shabbat candlelighting.

BACKGROUND:

In this, the second session of the course, the participants will begin to share their experiences and ask the questions which will make up the bulk of class discussion. Unlike the first session, during this lesson you want to encourage them to ask as many questions as they have and spend the time necessary to answer them fully. Many of the questions dealing with specific actions such as candlelighting are asked and answered in the student text. You will want to reinforce these answers during the class session in addition to providing the opportunity for practice of the first ritual actions of the Shabbat Seder.

GOALS:

1. Participants will share their reactions to the Shabbat home visit or information about the status of the Shabbat dinner observance in their own homes.

2. Participants will learn about the preparations necessary for creating a Shabbat Seder in the home.

3. Participants will discuss the place of *tzedakah* in the Shabbat Seder experience and practice this part of the observance.

4. Participants will discuss the meaning of candlelighting before Shabbat, review the details concerning the time and method of lighting candles and practice the ritual of blessing the candles.

PREPARATION:

You will need to set up the classroom the same way it was arranged during the first session. You should set the table with a white tablecloth, flowers (optional), a *tzedakah* box, and candlesticks. Have a box of candles available, preferably the economy size which usually contains 72 utility candles. Don't forget matches; if possible, get long fireplace matches. Have extra change available in case anyone forgets to bring some for *tzedakah*. Have *kipot* for the men and, if desired, headcoverings for the women who want to use them.

You do not need the rest of the Shabbat Seder items. From this point on, you will be adding the appropriate items at each session in which you deal with the ritual in which they are used.

PROCEDURE:

PART ONE—SHARING

1. WELCOME

    Try to GREET your class members when they arrive. Ask them to put their name tags on once again. This will help them identify their classmates during the sharing.

2. SHARING

    TELL them that you would like to begin the class by letting those who wish to share reactions to their Shabbat home visits do so. OPEN the floor for discussion, but ASK them to keep their descriptions and comments brief. DO NOT FORCE anyone to share. If they did not go on a home visit, suggest that they discuss Shabbat in their own home. This is more "threatening" than describing another family's home, but some of them may be anxious to share this information. Take 10-15 minutes for this part of the session.

PART TWO—HAKHANAH L'SHABBAT

In this lesson we will begin with CONCEPTS, then look at the OBJECTS involved and finish with the actual PRACTICE.

1. INTRODUCE the concept of *Hakhanah L'Shabbat* with an analogy to hosting a dinner party in your own home. SAY something like: "Shabbat doesn't just happen. It has to be prepared for. It's as if you were having people over to the house for a formal dinner party. I doubt whether you would be walking into the house a half hour before the guests were due to arrive and begin your preparations. No, the party must be planned well in advance; the tables must be set, the decorations prepared, the food ready, etc. The same thing goes for the Shabbat."

2. TEACH them that one of the interesting things about the Jewish calendar is the naming of the days of the week. The days are called by number. For example, Wednesday is *"Yom Rivi'i L'Shabbat"*—the fourth day to Shabbat. *"Yom Rishon L'Shabbat"* is the first day to Shabbat—Sunday. Friday is called *"Yom Shishi L'Shabbat"*—the sixth day to Shabbat. "To Shabbat" literally means "to the *next* Shabbat, the Shabbat to come." In the Jewish mind, every day anticipates the next Shabbat.

3. REVIEW the things necessary to think about in preparation for Shabbat. Are you having guests? What is on the menu? Who will do the marketing? Do I need to stop at the butcher shop? Will I bake or pick up *hallah*? Should I stop on the way home to pick up flowers? When will the house get cleaned?

4. DISCUSS the necessity to apportion the preparations among family members. In some families, each member has a specific role in the preparation for Shabbat. Give examples. In my family, the husband picks up the *hallah*, the wife cooks dinner, and the children set the table.

5. RECOGNIZE that preparing for Shabbat is difficult given the time schedules with which we live. It is not like Israel when everything closes up at noon so people can prepare to welcome the Shabbat. ACKNOWLEDGE that for many, Shabbat will be greeted as soon as everyone rushes into the house Friday evening. Nevertheless, some families arrange their schedules to ensure the proper preparations are done.

6. INTRODUCE the two reasons for "preparing for Shabbat." (1) **according to Jewish law, it is forbidden to engage in** *melakhah*—**work—on the Shabbat**. And (2) in order to honor Shabbat and embellish its celebration, preparation is needed.

   READ the fourth (Shabbat) commandment from the Ten Commandments in the text. POINT OUT two things: (1) the prohibition against work on the Shabbat applies to everyone and everything in the household. (2) there is no direct definition of the term *melakhah* in the Torah.

7. ALSO in the text are the 39 categories of work as defined by the Rabbis of the Talmud. These were the types of work done in building the *Mishkan*—the Tabernacle. Why were they chosen? Because even the building of the Tabernacle had to stop in order to honor Shabbat. In order to avoid transgressing the Shabbat by engaging in this work, the preparations had to be finished before Shabbat began.

8. Then, PRESENT the concept of *hiddur mitzvah*—the embellishment of a commandment. *Mitzvot* literally means commandments. This observance helps bring God into our lives as we identify ourselves with our people and the age old covenant of Israel. To embellish a commandment means to make it extra special or important. Shabbat is one of the weekly *mitzvot* which can be embellished in a variety of ways. Fresh flowers, white tablecloths, beautiful silver, china and crystal are all ways that Jews have made the celebration of Shabbat extra special.

9. INTRODUCE the concept of *TZEDAKAH*. POINT out that *tzedakah* does not mean "charity." Rather, it more closely means "righteous behavior," including the obligation to help others in need. We often express our concern with helping others by collecting money in *tzedakah* boxes, known in Yiddish as "pushkes." EXPLAIN that it became a tradition for the family to deposit a few coins in the *tzedakah* container just prior to initiating the Shabbat with candlelighting.

   SUGGEST that families can create their own personal *tzedakah* boxes out of jars or boxes or they can acquire one from any number of Jewish institutions, including the Jewish National Fund and the Women's League for Conservative Judaism. REMIND participants that when the box is full, the family should take it to the appropriate agency for counting. If the family has collected money using their own box, then when it is full, open and count the money (but not on Shabbat) and hold a discussion about where your family wants to distribute the funds.

10. SHOW the *tzedakah* box you brought to class. TELL the story of how and when you acquired it.

11. POINT OUT that the other objects which are used in the Shabbat Seder will be explained as you reach each step of the celebration.

12. PASS the *tzedakah* box and ask each person to contribute some coins. Provide them for those who may have forgotten to bring change.

13. REVIEW the points in the text about the procedures involved in giving *tzedakah* before candlelighting. TAKE the box from the table and put it on a chair or nearby counter. EXPLAIN that since using money is forbidden on Shabbat, it would be inappropriate to keep the box on the Shabbat table. So, before lighting candles, the box should be removed to another place, not to be touched after Shabbat begins.

14. READ AND DISCUSS the STUDY TEXTS in the textbook if time permits. Each chapter of the text has a selection of Study Texts. The participants will read these texts as part of their assignment each week. IF you find that the people in your class are "advanced," that is, they know something about the various ritual practices and may even know how to chant

the blessings already, you will not need as much time for practicing the prayers and rituals. FILL IN this time with a DIS-CUSSION of the Study Texts. If you have a class of beginners, you will not have time to discuss these texts. Simply POINT OUT their presence in the textbook and SUGGEST their use as Shabbat study material.

PART THREE—HADLAKAT NEROT

CONCEPTS

1. DISCUSS the significance of light as a Jewish symbol. ASK for examples of types of Jewish light, including *Hanukkah* lights, the *Ner Tamid* in the synagogue, and the *Yahrzeit* candle.

2. DESCRIBE the days when there was no electricity and it was critical to prepare the light before Shabbat so as not to trans-gress the Sabbath laws by lighting fire. In fact, the light was to be placed in the room where dinner was to be held. More-over, the lights must last at least as long as the dinner. POINT OUT that some of our most basic rituals had very practical beginnings.

OBJECTS

1. **CANDLESTICKS.** INTRODUCE the requirements for candlesticks. NOTE that although two candlesticks is the traditional minimum, according to Jewish law even one candle will suffice. SUGGEST the practice of many families to light one candle for each member of the family. EMPHASIZE that the two candles usually lit are taken to represent the two versions of the Shabbat commandment found in the Ten Commandments: "*Zachor*" (Remember) the Shabbat day to keep it holy (Exo-dus 20.8) and "*Shamor*" (Observe) the Shabbat day to keep it holy (Deuteronomy 5.12).

   ASK participants who brought candlesticks to class to tell a short story about them—where they got them, who gave them to the family, what was the occasion, etc. If you have many people who want to share their stories, limit each person to a minute or less.

2. **CANDLES.** SHOW participants the standard utility candles used for candlelighting. TELL them that it is okay to use long tapers, as long as they last through the dinner meal. White is the traditional color to be used. POINT OUT your box of econ-omy size candles and recommend that they purchase candles in bulk to avoid running out.

3. **MATCHES.** SUGGEST the use of long fireplace matches for lighting candles, especially in homes with young children. By using the long matches, small children can hold onto the match to help the adult lighting the candles.

PRACTICE

1. **THE BLESSING.** TRANSLATE THE BLESSING. TURN to the candlelighting blessing in the text. Explain that there are three columns of text from right to left: the Hebrew text is in the far right column, the English translation is in the next column, the English transliteration of the Hebrew is in the third column, and the step-by-step procedure for the ritual is the far left column. TELL those who can read Hebrew to follow the Hebrew and English translation columns. TELL those who cannot read Hebrew to follow the transliteration and translation columns. TRANSLATE the Hebrew blessing word-by-word.

   Since this is the first time you will engage in this translation process with the students, we will outline our suggested proce-dure explicitly:

Line 1

Barukh	means "blessed" or "praised." It comes from the Hebrew word *b'rakhah* which means "blessing" or "praise." *Barukh, b'rakhah*—hear the similarity?
attah	is the Hebrew word for "you." *Barukh attah*—praised are You—You meaning God.
Adonai	is one of the names of God. It isn't actually the name of God; according to tradition, the real name of God may not be pronounced. So, we have a variety of substitute names for God. *Adonai* is one of them; it is usually translated as "Lord."

Line 2

Eloheinu	is another name of God; in this case, it is translated "Our God"—the "*nu*" ending indicates the first person plural.
melekh	is the word for "Ruler" or "King."
ha'olam	is the word for the "universe."

THEN SAY: Let's review the first part: *"Barukh attah Adonai"*—"Praised are You, Lord,"—*"Eloheinu, melekh ha-olam"*—"Our God, Ruler of the Universe.

Let's continue.

Line 3

asher   is a transitional word meaning "which" or "who."

kidshanu   is related from the word *kadosh* which means "holy" or "sanctified." You have probably heard many words that sound like *kidshanu: kaddish*, as in Mourner's *Kaddish; kiddush*, as in the Shabbat *Kiddush*. Again, the "*nu*" ending makes the root refer to the first person plural— *kidshanu* literally means "He made us holy."

b'mitzvotav   is built from the word *mitzvot. Mitzvot* means "commandments." It is the plural of *mitzvah*. The "*B*" is a Hebrew conjunction meaning "through." The "*av*" ending indicates third person singular—"his." So, *b'mitzvotav* literally means "through His commandments."

Line 4

v'tzivanu   also comes from the same root as *mitzvah*—commandment. "*V*" is a Hebrew conjunction for "and" and the "*nu*" ending we already learned is what? (Someone should answer "us.") So, *v'tzivanu* literally translated is "and commanded us."

l'hadlik   is the word for "to kindle."

ner   is the word for "candle" (or "lamp").

shel   is the Hebrew word for "of."

Shabbat   you should know means "the Sabbath." So, *ner shel Shabbat means* "the Sabbath light."

Reviewing line 4: *v'tzivanu l'hadlik ner shel Shabbat*: "and commanded us to kindle the Shabbat light."

Now, let's try it in the Hebrew. Begin with line 1. Repeat after me:

Barukh attah Adonai—(have them repeat after you)

Eloheinu melekh ha-olam

asher kidshanu b'mitzvotav

v'tzivanu l'hadlik ner shel Shabbat.

2.   TEACH the tune for chanting the candlelighting blessing, line-by-line. Begin with line 1 and sing the tune at least once. Have the participants repeat after you, at least twice. YOU sing along with them as they practice. Go on to line 2. You sing it first, followed by the participants repeating line 2 at least twice. RETURN to line 1 and sing lines 1 and 2 together. GO to line 3. You sing it first, followed by the participants repeating line 3 at least twice. RETURN to line 1 and sing lines 1, 2 and 3. GO to line 4. You sing it first, followed by the participants repeating line 4 after you at least twice. RETURN to the beginning and practice the entire chanting through line 4.

Some participants may notice that you do not sing "Amen" at the conclusion of the blessing. POINT OUT that this is because "Amen" literally means "so be it" and developed as a method for those who did not know how to say the blessings to participate by stating their assent to whatever the blessing said. If you are saying the blessing yourself, saying "Amen" is superfluous.

ASK for any questions or parts people want repeated.

3.   DEMONSTRATE the proper way to light the candles. OUTLINE each step in the process as follows:

a)   PLACE candles in candlesticks. It is okay to burn the bottom of the candles a bit to allow some wax to drip into the candle receptacle on the stick. This helps keep the candles stationary in the stick.

b)   LIGHT the candles. The order is not important. Make sure that the fire catches the entire wick *before* you start the blessing.

c)   BLOW out the match.

d)   CIRCLE both hands over the flames three times. Most people begin the circling motion with hands spread out wide, bringing them over the flames and towards the body. This motion is repeated three times, ending with the hands in one of three possible positions: (1) covering the eyes with palms facing the eyes, (2) covering the eyes with palms facing out away from the body, or (3) placed in front of the candles, palms out, blocking the flames from view. Any of these three positions are acceptable, as long as the candles cannot be seen.

e) CHANT the blessing. Do not say "Amen" at the end of the blessing.

f) PAUSE for a few seconds with eyes still covered to say a private prayer. Then, slowly REMOVE your hands from the eyes, deliberately LOOK at the candles, and SAY "Shabbat Shalom."

g) GIVE everyone in the class a "Shabbat kiss" or handshake. It is very important for you to model this behavior. ENCOURAGE the participants to join you in wishing everyone in the class a Shabbat Shalom in the same manner. This will loosen up the group considerably. Make it a regular part of every practice of candlelighting.

4. PRACTICE the candlelighting procedure. Those participants who remembered to bring their candlesticks and candles should be given a chance to practice the lighting and the chanting of the blessing. INVITE the others to share the candlesticks around the table and practice as well, even though they may not have candles to light.

5. REVIEW the "Practical Questions and Answers" section of the learner's text. Of particular interest will be the discussion of the correct time for Shabbat candlelighting. This is one of the more difficult moments in the teaching of this material. According to Jewish law, candles may not be lit after the official candlelighting time 18 to 20 minutes before sundown. You should assert the importance of this part of the Shabbat Seder, pointing out that it is designed to avoid the desecration of the Shabbat which would result from lighting them after sundown.

Inevitably, you will find participants who will find it difficult to light candles at the correct time. Problems of leaving work early now face not only men, but working women as well. The problem of what to do during the short days of November and December when candlelighting times can be as early as 4:00 PM is a major concern. Some will tell you that whatever the *halakhah* says, they do not feel like it is Shabbat unless they begin the Shabbat dinner with candles, no matter what time it is. As with the rest of the material you will teach, people will take what is there and make it their own. But, it is one thing to be sympathetic to the difficulties and another to approve the violation of Jewish law.

Your position must be to assert that candles are lit at the official time. POINT OUT the various options families have devised to make sure candles are lit at the official time, even when Shabbat comes early. Certainly, having one family member light candles early before the others get home is not as nice as lighting with everyone gathered together. But you can point out that traditionally, the father and some of the children were hardly ever present at candlelighting since they were at the synagogue welcoming Shabbat while the mother had her private moment with the candles.

As with any other Jewish practice, we cannot control what people decide to do. The best we can do is to assert the legal requirements, present options within the *halakhah*, and encourage compliance.

ASSIGNMENTS

1. ASK participants to bring their candlesticks and candles again to the next session for practice.

2. INSTRUCT participants to read the chapters in the Learner's Text on *Shalom Aleikhem* and *Birkot ha-Mishpahah*.

3. ENCOURAGE participants to have their own Shabbat Seder at home on the coming Friday night. If they were at a host family the Friday night before this session, the coming Friday night may be their first opportunity to begin a Shabbat observance at home. SUGGEST that they begin with the basics: *candlelighting, Kiddush, ha-Motzi* over *hallah,* and perhaps a one line or paragraph *Birkat ha-Mazon (hazan et ha-kol).* Even starting just with candlelighting is at least a start. RECOGNIZE that they may feel somewhat uncomfortable with the ritual the first few times around. ASSURE them that the coming sessions will afford them an opportunity to practice every part of the Shabbat Seder each time you meet.

4. WISH everyone a "Shabbat Shalom."

Session 3 Outline

OVERVIEW:

In this lesson, participants (1) review the two previous lessons, (2) learn to chant *Shalom Aleikhem*, (3) to bless their children, and (4) to exchange prayers for each spouse.

BACKGROUND:

This session is about angels and families. The traditional hymn of greeting the Shabbat, *Shalom Aleikhem*, is a lovely way to set the mood for the table rituals to come. It is based on an ancient rabbinic tradition and the hymn is well known.

The series of blessings for family members which we call *Birkot ha-Mishpahah* is a compilation of the traditional blessings for children and the wife, plus suggested additions to include all family members. Anyone confronting the tradition at this point must understand the philosophical underpinnings which guided the development of the blessings for children and the wife in the middle ages. In a day and age when children were the hope for the future, the weekly blessing by the father was a very special moment indeed. The home was very much the domain of the woman in those days. The choice of *Eishet Hayil* from Proverbs as the prayer for the wife was quite appropriate given the prevailing view of the role of women then. Today, it is somewhat controversial in the light of feminism. Our research found some families retain it, some have dropped it from their observance and others have substituted new translations or even new alternative prayers. Moreover, some families have added parallel prayers for the husband in an attempt to include everyone. Other families have decided to use an all-inclusive family prayer in lieu of individual prayers for the wife and husband.

Your task in this session will be to describe the traditional prayers, emphasizing the blessings for the children. We have included the *Eishet Hayil*, a parallel Psalm for the husband and a family prayer. After discussing the issue with the group, participants will be encouraged to decide for themselves which of the options seems comfortable to them.

GOALS:

1. Participants will review the Shabbat Seder ritual to this point.

2. Participants will learn the background, the meaning of *Shalom Aleikhem* and how to chant it.

3. Participants will learn how to bless their children using the traditional formulae.

4. Participants will discuss the issues involved in prayers for the wife and husband and learn a variety of alternatives for possible inclusion in their own observance of the Shabbat Seder.

PREPARATION:

For this session, your table set-up will include everything you have used until now: white tablecloth, flowers (optional), a *tzedakah box*, candlesticks and candles, and matches. You will not need anything else specifically for teaching *Shalom Aleikhem* and *Birkot ha-Mishpahah* other than the student text.

PROCEDURE:

PART ONE—SHARING

1. WELCOME. Every session should begin with a warm welcome. You may want to invite participants to get a cup of coffee as they sit down. By now, people should feel comfortable in class, kibbitzing with you and their classmates.

2. SHARING. It is extremely important to begin each class session with a sharing session. SAY: "Would anyone like to volunteer to tell us about their Shabbat last week?" ENCOURAGE them to share something new they tried, or a problem that came up, or to ask a question of clarification about something already discussed in class. LIMIT this discussion to no more than ten minutes.

PART TWO—REVIEW

1. REVIEW every step of the Shabbat Seder you have learned thus far. EMPHASIZE the names of each step as you do. SAY: "The first thing we do is *Hakhanah L'Shabbat* which means _____?" Let participants try to fill in the answers to reinforce their knowledge of the names of the Shabbat Seder steps. ASK: "What is involved in *Hakhanah L'Shabbat*?" CALL ON someone to answer. Be sure that preparation includes *tzedakah*.

2. PASS the *tzedakah box* and have participants contribute coins. (By now, they should know to bring some change.) TAKE

the *tzedakah* box away from the table when finished.

3. ASK for the next step in the Seder. Someone should answer *"Hadlakat Nerot."* Participants should have brought their candlesticks to the session. SET UP candles for lighting and REVIEW the steps in the ritual very explicitly, just as you did during the last session. LIGHT candles and chant the blessing. If necessary, practice the blessing once or twice to help the people become more comfortable with it. If some participants forgot their candlesticks, ask them to share with a neighbor. ASK if there are any questions of clarification about *Hadlakat Nerot.*

4. ENCOURAGE participants to practice candlelighting on their own and to light candles every Friday evening.

PART THREE—SHALOM ALEIKHEM

CONCEPTS

1. BEGIN: *Shalom Aleikhem* is about ANGELS, "ministering angels" who enter the household at the beginning of Shabbat. READ the Talmudic legend cited in the text and recommend it for reading to families with young children. We even have a tradition in our family that the shadows from the candles on the ceiling are the angels themselves. For young children, this heightens the impact of the story.

2. INTRODUCE HOSPITALITY as the second theme of *Shalom Aleikhem.* In Hebrew, the term for hospitality is *Hakhnasat Orhim.* REVIEW the long tradition of hospitality in Jewish history. CITE Abraham welcoming strangers into his tent, the *Ha Lahma Anya* prayer in the *Pesah* Seder and the welcoming of wayfarers at the synagogue. For many Jews, Shabbat wouldn't be Shabbat without a guest at the table.

    POINT out that traditionally Friday night synagogue services are held before dinner. Fathers and sons would go to the synagogue for *Minha, Kabbalat Shabbat* and *Ma'ariv* services. There they might see a stranger in need of a place to go for Shabbat dinner. It was unthinkable to let a stranger leave the synagogue alone. So, an invitation would be extended and the family and guest(s) would return to the home to begin the Shabbat Seder. By the way, the woman of the house was usually prepared in advance for this eventuality.

    The tradition of inviting family and friends to the Shabbat dinner celebration is very strong and should be encouraged. Many of the families we spoke to emphasized how often they have guests at their Shabbat table. In fact, many stated how much easier it is to get the cooperation of their children to participate in the Shabbat Seder when guests are at the table.

PRACTICE

1. TURN to the text of *Shalom Aleikhem* in the student book. Again, SUGGEST that those who know Hebrew work with the Hebrew and English columns. Those who need the transliteration should work with that column and the English column. With a long text like this, SUGGEST that participants take a piece of paper and mask down the text line by line as you review it with them.

2. TEACH the Hebrew and translation of *Shalom Aleikhem*:

Line 1

Shalom Aleikhem	*shalom* means "peace" or "welcome." *Aleikhem* is a combination of the preposition *alei* meaning "upon" and *khem* meaning "you" (second person plural).
malakhei	is the plural of *malakh*—"angels."
ha-shareit	is the adjective describing the angels. It means "ministering".

PRACTICE the entire line in Hebrew

Line 2

malakhei elyon	*Malakhei*—angels, is the same word as in line 1, and *elyon*—which means "Most High" referring to God. So, *malakhei elyon* translates to "angels of the Most High."

Line 3

mimelekh	is a combination of the preposition *mi* which means "from" and *melekh* which is the word for Ruler. In this case referring to God as "Ruler."
malkhei	is from the same word as *melekh*, "Ruler." NOTICE it is **not** the same word as *malakhei*—"angels."
	POINT OUT the difference in Hebrew is an *"aleph."*

ha-melakhim	is the plural form of *melekh*—"Rulers." *Ha* means "the".
	All together, the line reads "*mimelekh malkhei ha-melakhim*"—"from the Ruler, the Ruler of Rulers."

Line 4.

Ha-kadosh barukh hu	is a name of God. Literally it means "the Holy One, praised is He." *Ha-kadosh* is from the same root word, *kadosh*, as *kaddish* and *kiddush*. Remember *kidshanu* from the candlelighting blessing? Same word. *Ha-kadosh* means "the Holy One," referring to God. *Barukh* is a familiar term; it means "praised" or "blessed." *Hu* is the Hebrew pronoun for "He," referring to God.

REPEAT this procedure for each of the next three stanzas. POINT OUT that with the exception of the first line of each stanza, the words are exactly the same as the first stanza. Therefore, EMPHASIZE each stanza's first line.

In Stanza 2, the first line (**line 5** in the text) begins

Bo'akhem	meaning "you come." The "you" refers to the angels of peace.
l'shalom	means "in peace."
malakhei	means "angels."
ha-shalom	*ha-shalom* means "peace." Notice that the adjective describing the angels changes in this line from *ha-shareit* to *ha-shalom*. So, the line reads: "Come in peace, angels of peace." The rest of the stanza is the same as stanza 1.

In Stanza 3, **line 9** begins

Barkhuni	which is a form of the familiar word *barukh*. It means "bless me." The rest of the line is exactly the same as line 5.
l'shalom	means "with peace" and
malakhei ha-shalom	means "angels of peace." The line thus is: "Bless me with peace, angels of peace." POINT OUT that most Jewish liturgy is in the first person plural—"we." Here is an unusual instance of the first person singular—asking for personal blessings from the angels. The remainder of the stanza is exactly the same as that of the previous two stanzas.

The last stanza begins

Tzeitkhem	which means "you go out." Add
l'shalom	and you have "you go out in peace." Who should go out or leave?
malakhei ha-shalom	"the angels of peace." Here, we are wishing the angels a peaceful departure when the end of Shabbat comes. The remainder of the last stanza is exactly the same as the previous three stanzas.

REVIEW the meaning of the entire *Shalom Aleikhem*. It begins by welcoming the ministering angels, the messengers of the Most High, with peace. Then, it prays that the coming of the angels of peace will be in peace. We then ask for the personal blessing of the angels. Finally, we hope that the departure of the angels of peace will be in peace.

3. SING the hymn once through yourself. ASK the participants to listen or to sing along quietly. Many of the people will have heard this famous song, so it should not be difficult for them to catch on rapidly. REPEAT the song a second time and ASK the participants to join in. With all the repetition, you will probably only need to sing it through once or, at most, twice. SING SLOWLY and DELIBERATELY, emphasizing the correct pronunciation of the Hebrew. You will be able to pick up the pace later. On your last time through, INVITE the participants to join hands and sway with the music.

4. *Shalom Aleikhem* can be sung either standing or sitting. It is completely up to individual preference.

5. REMIND the people that you will be reviewing the song at each of the coming sessions. ENCOURAGE them to listen to the tape and practice at home. SUGGEST that as they become more comfortable with it, they can add *Shalom Aleikhem* to their own Shabbat Seder celebration.

PART FOUR—BIRKOT HA-MISHPAḤAH

CONCEPTS

1. INTRODUCE the concept of SHALOM BAYIT. It literally means "a complete home." DIFFERENTIATE the meaning of *pax*

(Latin for "peace," meaning "quiet") and *shalom* which comes from the Hebrew root *shalem*—"complete" or "whole." This is truly a dynamic concept of family harmony—a goal not easily achieved. On the other hand, family after family reports that this section of the Shabbat Seder represents a weekly opportunity for the family to come together, to appreciate each other, to bless each other. Even when relationships are tense after a bad week, this ritual allows family members the chance for healing, for the sharing of basic love and appreciation. It is an unusually significant moment in the Shabbat Seder.

2. EXPLAIN: The BLESSING OF THE CHILDREN is rooted in a very old tradition in Judaism, dating back to Isaac's blessing his sons. TELL THEM THAT the formula for blessing sons refers to Jacob's grandchildren, Ephraim and Menasheh, who, despite the attractions of assimilating into the Egyptian society ruled by their father Joseph, maintained their Jewish identities. EXPLAIN: This can be a powerful lesson for us today as we face widespread assimilation.

    The girls are asked to be like the four ancestral mothers of Judaism: Sarah—a woman of courage, Rebecca—the biblical model of hospitality, and Rachel and Leah—loyal sisters.

    EXPLAIN THAT the blessings for the children conclude with the ancient "Priestly Benediction," the same formula which was recited by the High Priests in the Temple. This is an echo to the Temple service. Parents preside over the Shabbat table just as the Priests presided over the altar in the Temple.

3. POINT OUT that THE BLESSING OF THE WIFE and THE BLESSING OF THE HUSBAND is a natural conclusion to this series of family blessings.

    TELL THEM that traditionally, the husband recited the *Eishet Ḥayil* to his wife. ACKNOWLEDGE that these verses from Proverbs have become problematic for some women in the light of feminist sensitivities. If you look carefully at the translations of the prayer, it is not difficult to imagine what bothers many women. On the other hand, some women really love this traditional form of praise and acknowledgement.

    REMEMBER: Our approach is to present the traditional formulation, as well as a parallel prayer for the husband. In the end, as with the blessings for the children, here is a wonderful opportunity for husband and wife to share a moment of closeness together, regardless of the formulation ultimately decided upon.

PRACTICE

1. TURN to the Blessings for the Children in the textbook.

Line 1

Y'simkha	comes from the Hebrew root *sim* meaning "to make." The *yud* or "y" sound stands for the indirect command form for "he" in Hebrew. The *kha* ending means "you" (second person masculine singular). Together, *y'simkha* means "(may) He make you."
Elohim	is a name of God. So, line 1 translated is "(May) God make you."
	BEWARE the gutteral sounds; have the people drill it.

Line 2

k'Efrayim	The *k'* stands for the preposition "like" or "as." *Efrayim* is Hebrew for Ephraim, a son of Joseph in the Bible.
v'khiMenashe	is a combination of three word-parts: *v'* in Hebrew means "and," *khi* means "like" or "as" (it is the same as *k'* above—its place in the word makes it sound different), and *Menashe* is the word for Menasseh, another son of Joseph.
	All together, line 2 translates: "like Ephraim and Menasseh." The entire blessing for sons translated is "(May) God make you like Ephraim and Menasseh."
	PRACTICE the entire blessing for the sons at least twice.

2. The blessing for daughters begins on **line 3**.

Y'simeikh	is the feminine form for "(May) He make you." The *eikh* ending is second person feminine singular.
Elohim	is a name of God.
	So, line 3 translated is "(May) God make you."

Line 4

k'Sarah	which means "like Sarah."
	The rest of the line lists the other ancestral mothers:
Rivka	Rebecca
Raḥel	Rachel
v'Leah	and Leah.
	Practice the entire blessing for the daughters at least twice.

3. The ancient words of the Priestly Benediction conclude the blessings for the children. BEGIN on **line 5**. (**BEWARE the Hebrew of this section**. It is very difficult to get. The gutterals are hard to master and you must speak very slowly and carefully. These words will need more practice than the others.)

Line 5

Y'varekh'kha	has a root word which is familiar: *barukh*—bless. The Hebrew form here combines the *y'* which indicates third person masculine singular indirect command—"let him," and the *kha* ending which indicates second person masculine singular—"you." (Although the intent of the "you" here is for all the children, in Hebrew, if both males and females are referred to in one word, the masculine form is used.)
Adonai	is a name of God which is usually translated "Lord." So, *Y'varekh'kha Adonai* means "(May) the Lord bless you."
v'yishm'rekha	The *v'* stands for "and." *Y'shm're* comes from the root word *shomer* meaning "guard" or "watch over." The *kha* ending should be familiar by now—it means "you." Together, *v'yishm'rekha* means "and watch over you."
	Thus, line 5 fully translated is "(May) the Lord bless you and watch over you." PRACTICE line 5 at least twice.

Line 6

Ya'er	comes from the Hebrew word *or* meaning "light." In this form, *ya'er* means "(may) He shine."
Adonai	is a name of God.
panav	means "His face."
elekha	is a Hebrew preposition meaning "toward you."
viḥuneka	is a combination word. *Vi* means "and," the root word is *ḥen* meaning "grace" and the *ka* ending indicates second person masculine singular "you." Together, *viḥuneka* means "and be gracious to you."
	Line 6 altogether means "(May) the Lord cause His face to shine upon you and be gracious to you." PRACTICE line 6 at least twice.

The last sentence of the Priestly Benediction takes two lines.

Line 7

Yisa	is the Hebrew for "Let Him lift up."
Adonai	is a name of God.
panav	is the same word for "His face" as in line 6, as is
elekha	"toward you."
	So, line 7 translated is "(May) the Lord lift up His face toward you."
	Practice line 7 at least twice.

Line 8

v'yasem	which means "and let Him place (or give)."
l'kha	is another preposition meaning "to you."
shalom	means "peace."
	Together, line 8 translated means: "And (may) He give you peace." PRACTICE line 8 at least twice.
	TRANSLATE lines 7 and 8 together: "(May) the Lord lift up His face toward you and (may) He give you peace."

REVIEW the entire Priestly Benediction (lines 5-8) at least twice. Stop at difficult words and practice them until most of the participants seem to get it. PRACTICE all the blessings for the children at least once before leaving the Hebrew.

2. ENCOURAGE the participants to practice the Hebrew for the blessings for the children at home using the tape. RECOGNIZE that the Hebrew is very difficult. TELL them that they may choose to read these prayers in the English, but you want them to try to master the Hebrew. For those for whom the Hebrew is simply too difficult to say, even using the transliteration, it will better to have them do the prayers in English than to give them up altogether.

3. DISCUSS the "Practical Questions and Answers" about blessing the children found in the textbook. REVIEW them for yourself before class and highlight the points most interesting to you. Participants may have questions from their own reading of the text. BE PREPARED to answer them.

4. DEMONSTRATE the procedure for blessing the children. PICK one male class member to be "your child" and demonstrate the blessing by PLACING your hands upon his head and reciting the blessing. DO the same with a female class member, reciting the appropriate blessing. Conclude with the Priestly Benediction over BOTH.

5. ASK class members to pair off and practice the blessings. LEAD them in the prayers—first the blessings for the sons, then the daughters, and end with the Priestly Benediction.

6. TURN to the *Eishet Hayil* in the textbook. Before class, YOU will have decided whether you will be teaching it in Hebrew or English. Unless your class lasts longer than six sessions, our recommendation is to teach the *Eishet Hayil* in English. The Hebrew is difficult and unless someone is already fluent in Hebrew, you will not have time to teach the Hebrew text. It is on the tape and you can refer participants to that if they get to the point where they want to be able to recite *Eishet Hayil* in Hebrew. EXPLAIN your decision to the group.

7. Assuming you are teaching the *Eishet Hayil* in English, ASK all the men in the class to read the prayer in the English. If there are no men in class, ask all the women to read it. You will probably hear some snickers as the text is read. DISCUSS why people laugh at these words or feel uncomfortable reading them.

   SUGGEST that here is a chance for the husband to turn to his wife and praise her. If the words don't resonate with either you or your spouse, SUGGEST that the couple may find an alternative reading to insert here or they may want to use the family prayer found in the textbook.

8. SUGGEST that it may be appropriate for the family to include a parallel prayer of praise for the husband. Many families have adopted Psalm 112 for this purpose. ASK all the women in your group to recite Psalm 112 outloud. ELICIT their feelings about saying these words. ASK the men in the group how they would feel about hearing these words each week from their wife.

9. DON'T FORGET KISSING. It is very important to suggest that spouses kiss each other after reciting these prayers. SAY: "You've heard of 'sealed with a kiss?' Well, here's a chance to put it into practice!" or some other clever comment.

10. REVIEW the "Practical Questions and Answers" about the prayers for the wife and husband. BE SENSITIVE to single parents in your group. SUGGEST that in their case, the children may be asked to recite the appropriate prayer if they are old enough. OR, SUGGEST the use of the Family Prayer included in the textbook. EMPHASIZE that this part of the Shabbat Seder should be a series of personal moments between parents and children and husbands and wives. Personal words added to the traditional blessings are entirely appropriate and will be much appreciated. This is your time together. Make it count!

ASSIGNMENTS

The assignment for next session is to read the section in the text on the *Kiddush*. As usual, part of the assignment is to have a Shabbat Seder at home. Items to bring to the next session: *tzedakah* money, candlesticks and candles, the textbook, and *Kiddush* cups.

Session 4 Outline

OVERVIEW:

In this session, participants (1) review previous lessons and (2) learn the meaning of the Shabbat evening *Kiddush* and how to chant it.

BACKGROUND:

The *Kiddush* is the central prayer of the Shabbat Seder. In it, we sanctify the Shabbat day—we pronounce the holiness of the day. This was derived from a revolutionary view in the history of religion, namely that God alone is holy, that all things—places and people—are holy in so far as they derive this holiness from God. Thus, the Temple in Jerusalem was holy because God consecreated it with the Divine presence. Similarly, the Shabbat is holy because God declared it to be so. The *Kiddush* is an acknowledgement of this and witnesses our desire to share in the holiness of the day.

The *Kiddush* is not simply a prayer over wine. Wine is only symbolic of the joy we feel as we experience the holiness of Shabbat. The text of the *Kiddush* focuses on two major events in the history of the Jewish people: the creation of the world and the Exodus from Egypt. Each embodied a Shabbat-like experience. At creation, God created the first Shabbat as a Divine day of rest. At the Exodus, God brought the Israelites out of slavery and into a life of freedom and rest, a kind of Shabbat. The Shabbat *Kiddush* is a weekly reminder of these two seminal events.

GOALS:

1. Participants will review the Shabbat Seder ritual to this point.

2. Participants will learn the meaning of the *Kiddush* and how to chant it.

3. Participants will be able to explain that the *Kiddush* is the expression of two themes: Creation and the Exodus.

PREPARATION:

For this session, your table set-up will include everything you have used until now: white tablecloth, flowers (optional), a *tzedakah* box, candlesticks and candles, and matches. You will need to bring a *Kiddush* cup and a bottle of Kosher wine, preferably Israeli. You should also have extra cups available for those people who forget to bring their own *Kiddush* cups.

PART ONE—SHARING

1. WELCOME. By now, you should be comfortable with everyone's name and they should be familiar with the classroom set-up.

2. SHARING. Always begin the formal class session with sharing by the participants. ASK them to share any stories about their Shabbat experiences at home. As you get further along in the course, more people should be willing to talk about their attempts to institute Shabbat rituals in their homes. They may have specific questions about things that are unclear or they may just want to share feelings about what is happening to them at home and in the class. ALLOW no more than ten minutes for this sharing.

PART TWO—REVIEW

1. REVIEW the Shabbat Seder up to this point. ASK the participants to list the various steps as you do them. PASS the *tzedakah* box for *Hakhanah L'Shabbat*, LIGHT the Shabbat candles and chant the blessing, SING *Shalom Aleikhem*, PRACTICE the *Birkot ha-Mishpahah*, including the blessings for children in Hebrew; *Eishet Ḥayil* and Psalm 112 for the parents.

2. EVALUATE where the people are having trouble. The earlier steps of the Seder, such as candlelighting, should be much easier for the participants following several opportunities to practice. Do not be surprised if the blessings for the children are difficult for them. They just learned it at the last session. Spend a few extra minutes reviewing the Hebrew for these blessings. REMIND them that the Hebrew gets easier with practice.

PART THREE—KIDDUSH

CONCEPTS

1. BEGIN with the word *Kiddush*. EXPLAIN that *Kiddush* comes from the Hebrew word *kadosh* which means "holy".

   POINT OUT that we have heard the word *kadosh* or derivatives of it many times in the Shabbat Seder already. The *Kiddush* prayer is the vehicle we use to proclaim the holiness of Shabbat.

EMPHASIZE that the *Kiddush* is not simply a prayer over wine. Wine is a symbol of the joy we experience in welcoming the Shabbat into the home. It was probably included in the *Kiddush* because of the influence of the Romans who always began a festive meal with a cup of wine. For us, the important part is not the wine. EXPLAIN THAT *Kiddush* can even be said over bread. The critical point is that we are setting aside the time of Shabbat as special when we recite the *Kiddush*.

2. READ the citation from Abraham Joshua Heschel. ELICIT participant's feelings about the way we waste time in our everyday lives. Try to help them understand how radically different the Jewish view of time is.

3. TURN to the *Kiddush* in the textbook. POINT OUT that there are three parts to the prayer: (1) the *Vayekhulu*—the introductory paragraph retelling God's creation of Shabbat; (2) the *Borei p'ri ha-gafen*—the blessing over the wine; and (3) the *M'kadesh ha-Shabbat*—the paragraph which recalls the two reasons for Shabbat and sanctifies it as holy time.

4. DISCUSS the two biblical references in the *Kiddush*: Creation and Exodus. (These are found at the end of the *Kiddush* chapter). The Creation is referred to in the opening paragraph of the *Kiddush*, the *Vayekhulu*, which is the actual biblical account of the creation of Shabbat.

   POINT OUT that Shabbat is called *zikaron l'ma'aseh v'reishit*—a remembrance of the work of creation—in the third paragraph of the *Kiddush*.

   AND THAT The Exodus is mentioned in the third paragraph also; it is referred to as *zekher litziyat Mitzrayim*—a remembrance of the Exodus from Egypt.

   Creation is an obvious theme. Why the Exodus? DISCUSS why the Exodus was a kind of Shabbat. Mention that during the week we are slaves to the work place, but on Shabbat we free ourselves from it. Also, MENTION the juxtaposition of the Exodus from Egypt and the creation of the Jewish people. It was after leaving Egypt that the Israelites received the Ten Commandments, one of which is to "remember the Shabbat to keep it holy," and became the Jewish people.

5. DISCUSS the third theme of *Kiddush*—the chosenness of the Jewish people. The concept of the Jews as a "chosen people" is one of the most misunderstood in Judaism. It is not an elitist notion. Rather, God chose the Jewish people with whom to make a covenant—a contract. It went something like this: if you Jewish people keep My laws, I will watch over you and make you a great nation. Some say the Jews chose God. There is a Midrash (a rabbinic story) which says that God took the Torah to every other people on earth offering it to them. But, each one found something in the Torah which was unacceptable. Ultimately, only the Jews agreed to accept and keep the laws of the Torah. We are only special in our obligation to guard the commandments, among them to observe the Shabbat.

OBJECTS

1. *KIDDUSH* CUP. INVITE participants to share their *Kiddush* cups with the group. ASK them to tell the story of the cup; how did they acquire it, when, from whom? We have included some stories from the families we interviewed which should give them the idea of what to share. REVIEW the requirements for a *Kiddush* cup as listed in the textbook.

2. WINE. Try to bring Kosher wine from Israel for purposes of demonstration. EMPHASIZE that the wine must be made from grapes. It is traditional to use red wine as well. ENCOURAGE the use of Israeli wine as a sign of support for the Jewish state. SUGGEST red grape juice for the children, although in many homes children learn to sip a bit of real wine for the *Kiddush*.

PRACTICE

1. TURN to the *Kiddush* in the textbook. REMIND participants that they may follow with the two right-hand columns if they can read Hebrew or with the transliteration and translation columns.

2. BEGIN the translation with the *Vayekhulu* paragraph. Practice each line of Hebrew at least twice.

Line 1

Vay'hi	the *v'* means "and" and *y'hi* means "there was."
erev	is the word for "evening."
vay'hi	repeats first word.
voker	(from the Hebrew *boker*) means "morning."
	Together, line 1 translates "And there was evening and there was morning."

Line 2

Yom	"day"

| *ha-shishi* | "the sixth." |

Together, *yom ha-shishi* means "the sixth day."

All together, lines 1 and 2 translated are: "And there was evening and there was morning: the sixth day." This is actually the last line of the last verse of Chapter 1 of Genesis which concludes with the creation of the sixth day.

The *Vayekhulu* itself consists of the first lines of Chapter 2 of Genesis.

Line 3

| *Vayekhulu* | is based on the Hebrew word for "finished" or "completed." The *va* means "and" and the *u* ending indicates third person plural "they." Together, *vayekhulu* means "and they were completed." |

The "they" is the next word.

| *ha-shamayim* | which means "the heavens." |

Together, line 3 translated is: "and the heavens were completed."

Line 4

V'ha-aretz	means "and the earth (literally "land");"
v'khol	means "and all;"
tz'va'am	is the Hebrew word for "components."

Together, lines 3 and 4 when translated grammatically into English would read: "And the heavens and the earth and all its components were completed."

REMIND the students that the linear translation is a bit stilted in English in order for them to see the word-to-word correspondence with the Hebrew.

Line 5

Vay'khal	is from the same root as *Vay'khulu* in line 3. In this case, it means "and He completed." The "He" is the next Hebrew word
Elohim	a name of God.
bayom	means "on the day."
ha-shvi'i	"the seventh."

Together, line 5 reads: "and God completed on the seventh day." What did God complete? Go to line 6.

Line 6

m'lakhto	"His work,"
asher	"which,"
asa	"He had been doing."

Line 7

| *Va'yishbot* | "and He ceased." HERE we have the root for Shabbat. POINT OUT that Shabbat doesn't mean "rest." It means "stop," "cease." |
| *bayom ha-shvi'i* | is the same as in line 5—"on the seventh day." |

Line 7 is: "and He ceased on the seventh day." What did He cease? Go on

Line 8

| *mikol* | "from all," |
| *m'lakhto* | "His work," from the word *melakhah*—labor which we discussed in the chapter on Shabbat preparation. |

asher	"which,"
asa	"He had done," (the exact same phrase from line 6, although we changed the translation of *asa* to emphasize the fact that God was done with His work).
	All together, lines 7 and 8 translated are: "And He ceased on the seventh day from all His work which He had done."

Lines 9-12 tell the rest of the story of what God did.

Line 9

Vay'varekh	a word from the root *barukh*—"bless." It literally means "and He blessed." Who blessed?
Elohim	a name of God. What did God bless?
et yom ha-shvi'i	"the seventh day."
	Together, line 9 is "And God blessed the seventh day."

Line 10

vay'kadesh oto	"And He sanctified it (the seventh day)." EMPHASIZE the root *kadosh*—"sanctify" or "made holy," for it will be the central thematic word in the rest of the *Kiddush*.
	Kiddush— *kadosh*, EMPHASIZE the connection.

Why did God sanctify the seventh day? Line 11 gives the answer.

Ki vo	"because on it,"
shavat	(The *Shabbat* "root word")—"He ceased,"
mikol m'lakhto	"from all His work" (same as in line 8).

Line 12

asher	"which,"
bara Elohim	"God had created,"
la'asot	"through doing."

NOW, RETURN to the top of the page and PRACTICE the entire *Vayekhulu* at least twice.

3. There are a number of tunes for *Vayekhulu*. We have included one on the accompanying audiotape. Depending upon how many sessions the course is scheduled for, you may want to teach a tune to this part of the *Kiddush*. However, if you are pressed for time, skip the tune and SUGGEST that participants recite the paragraph in Hebrew. If that seems too difficult, SUGGEST they read it in English as a preliminary to the more important paragraphs to come. In other words, the priority should be placed on learning to chant the *Borei p'ri ha-gafen* and the *M'kadesh ha-Shabbat*.

4. CONTINUE the translation with the *Borei p'ri ha-gafen*.

Line 1

Barukh	"praised,"
attah	"(are) You,"
Adonai	A name of God.

Line 2

Eloheinu	"our God,"
melekh ha-olam	"Ruler of the universe." The formula should be familiar from the candlelighting *b'rakhah*.

Line 3

Borei	"Creator" (from the word *bara*—"create"),
p'ri	"the fruit of,"

| *ha-gafen* | "the vine." |
| | All together, lines 1-3: "Praised are You, Adonai, Our God, Ruler of the Universe, Creator of the fruit of the vine." |

PRACTICE all the Hebrew words in lines 1-3 at least twice. TEACH the tune, line by line, repeating if necessary until everyone is able to sing the prayer.

Once the blessing over the wine is down pat, CONTINUE with the translation of the *M'kadesh ha-Shabbat*.

BEGIN with **lines 4 and 5**:

Barukh attah Adonai	"Praised are You, Adonai,"
Eloheinu melekh ha-olam	"Our God, Ruler of the universe"
	This should be quite familiar by now. PRACTICE the Hebrew once.

Line 6 (will sound familiar from *Hadlakat Nerot*)

Asher	"who,"
kidshanu	"sanctified us,"
b'mitzvotav	"through His commandments."
	EMPHASIZE *kidshanu*, another instance of the term *kadosh*.

Line 7

v'ratza	"and He is pleased,"
vanu	"with us."
	Together, "who sanctified us through His commandments and is pleased with us."
	PRACTICE the Hebrew in lines 6 and 7 once. Then, PRACTICE all the Hebrew words in lines 4-7 once.

Line 8

v'Shabbat kodsho	"and His holy Shabbat." Notice again the use of *kadosh*.
b'ahava	means "with love."
uv'ratzon	means "and satisfaction."
	Together: "and His holy Shabbat, with love and satisfaction."

Line 9

hinhilanu	"He gave us as an inheritance." The word comes from the Hebrew word *henhil* meaning "to give an inheritance" or "to bequeath."
	Lines 8 and 9 together read: "And His holy Shabbat, with love and satisfaction, He gave us as an inheritance."
	PRACTICE the Hebrew of lines 8 and 9

Line 10 names the Shabbat as a reminder of one of the major themes of the day.

zikaron	"a remembrance" (literally "a souvenir")
l'ma'asei	"of the work,"
v'reishit	"of Creation."

Line 11 describes the Shabbat as being the first among all the holidays.

| *Ki* | "for," |
| *hu* | "it," |

yom	"day,"
t'ḥilah	"first,"
l'mikra'ei kodesh	"the sacred days of assembly" (a biblical term referring to major holidays). Note the use of *kadosh* again.
	Together, "For it was first among the sacred days of assembly."

Line 12 states the second major theme of the *Kiddush*. Shabbat is:

zekher	"a rememberance" (similar to *zikaron*; CUE the word *Yizkor*—the service when we remember the dead),
litziyat	"the Exodus" (literally "going out"),
Mitzrayim	"(from) Egypt."
	Together: "a remembrance of the Exodus from Egypt." PRACTICE the Hebrew.

Line 13 introduces the notion of chosenness.

Ki	"For,"
vanu—	"us,"
vaḥarta	"You have chosen."
	Together: "For You have chosen us."

Line 14

V'otanu kidashta	"and You have sanctified us" (NOTICE *kadosh* again),
mikol ha-amim	"from all the peoples."
	Together: "And You have sanctified us from (among) all the peoples."

Line 15

V'Shabbat kodsh'kha	"and Your holy Shabbat" (Notice the form of *kadosh* again),
b'ahava uv'ratzon	"with love and satisfaction" (exactly the same as the phrase in line 8)

Line 16

hinḥaltanu	"You gave us as an inheritance" (a different form of the same word in line 9).
	Together: "and Your holy Shabbat with love and satisfaction, You gave us as an inheritace." PRACTICE all the Hebrew words . WATCH OUT for *hinḥaltanu*.

Lines 17 and 18 are the concluding blessing stating the overall theme:

Barukh	"Praised,"
attah	"(are) You,"
Adonai	a name of God,
m'kadesh	"Sanctifier," (another *kadosh*)
ha-Shabbat	"of the Shabbat."

PRACTICE the entire *M'kadesh ha-Shabbat*, lines 4-18 at least once. TEACH the tune for the *M'kadesh ha-Shabbat*, line by line. PRACTICE when necessary to make sure participants are able to sing the tune.

In our experience, many of the participants will be able to join at line 13, *ki vanu vaḥarta* since that is where the congregation usually joins in at the Friday night synagogue service when the Cantor chants the *Kiddush*. CONCENTRATE on the first part of *M'kadesh ha-Shabbat* until everyone appears to be able to sing it.

REINFORCE the major concept of the *Kiddush* by ASKING the participants to find how many times a form of *kadosh* is found in the *Kiddush*. The answer is 7: in the *Vayekhulu*—line 10 and in the *M'kadesh ha-Shabbat*, lines 6, 8, 11, 14, 15 and 18. REMIND them that the *Kiddush* sanctifies the·day of Shabbat, not the wine.

PRACTICE the singing of the *Kiddush* from *Borei p'ri ha-gafen* at least once before leaving the prayer. REMIND the people to practice it at home. SUGGEST they listen to the tape. EMPHASIZE that you want them to be comfortable with the singing of the *Kiddush*.

6. ASK the participants to stand. LIFT the *Kiddush* cup. Have them do likewise. PRACTICE the *Kiddush* from the beginning as if you were at the Shabbat table. ASK everyone to sing along. REMIND them that the tune is on the tape and ENCOURAGE them to practice at their next Friday night dinner, as well as once or twice during the week.

7. REVIEW the "Practical Questions and Answers" in the textbook. DISCUSS the issue of standing or sitting during the *Kiddush*. We suggest standing if there is no previous tradition in the family. DEMONSTRATE how to fill the cup with wine and how to hold the cup when chanting the *Kiddush*. TELL the participants that it is not necessary to say "Amen" at the end of the *Kiddush* for the same reasons we stated when this issue was discussed in the session on *Hadlakat Nerot*.

8. ASK if there are any questions about the *Kiddush*.

ASSIGNMENTS

1. ASK participants to bring their Shabbat ritual items again to the next session for the review. In addition, ASK those who may have washing cups and basins, and *hallah* plates, covers and knives to bring them.

2. REMIND participants to celebrate the coming Shabbat with a Shabbat Seder that is comfortable to their family. ENCOURAGE those who have begun with just the basics: candles, wine and *hallah*—to add something new: *Shalom Aleikhem*, or blessing the children, etc. This should be a time of experimentation, learning how to create a Shabbat Seder experience which will be meaningful to themselves and their families.

Session 5 Outline

OVERVIEW:

In this session, participants (1) review previous lessons, (2) learn the meaning and process of ritual hand-washing, (3) the breaking of the Shabbat *ḥallah* bread, and (4) how to organize the Shabbat meal.

BACKGROUND:

The *Netilat Yadayim* and *ha-Motzi* prayers are essentially preparation for the meal, the *Seudat Shabbat*. The ritual washing of hands is not limited to the Shabbat meal; it is required by Jewish law at every meal for which the *ha-Motzi* is recited. Our understanding of the ritual is as an echo to the ancient Temple service. Whether or not today's Jews will relate to this part of the service is a matter of conjecture. We present the *Netilat Yadayim* as an important part of the traditional Shabbat Seder ritual.

The process of breaking bread is an especially significant part of the table service. There is a special bread, *ḥallah*, which has its roots both in the biblical account of the manna God sent to the Israelites in the desert and in the Temple service once again. There is a special way to mark the bread for breaking. And, as we shall see, there are numerous ways to break the bread itself. As the last act before the *Seudat Mitzvah*, the "commanded meal," the *ha-Motzi* is a most anticipated part of the Shabbat Seder.

GOALS:

1. Participants will review the Shabbat Seder ritual to this point.

2. Participants will learn the meaning and the procedure for *Netilat Yadayim*—"washing the hands."

3. Participants will learn the meaning and the procedure for chanting the *ha-Motzi* and breaking the *ḥallah* bread.

4. Participants will discuss ways to prepare an especially festive Shabbat meal—a *Seudat Mitzvah*.

PREPARATION:

For this session, your table set-up will include everything you have used until now: white tablecloth, flowers (optional), a *tzedakah* box, candlesticks and candles, matches, *Kiddush* cup, and wine. You will also need a washing cup or pitcher, a basin, a towel, a *ḥallah* plate, a *ḥallah* cover, a *ḥallah* knife (optional), a regular plate, two whole *ḥallot*, and a salt shaker. You will also need a source of water: either a sink with faucet or a large container of water.

PART ONE—SHARING

1. WELCOME. At this point, you may have participants coming early to help you set up the class. Everyone should be quite comfortable with each other and you.

2. SHARING. Always begin the class with sharing by the participants. ASK them to share any stories or feelings about their on-going Shabbat experiments at home. Now that there is plenty for them to try out, you may have no trouble finding people willing to share. LIMIT the sharing to no more than ten minutes.

PART TWO—REVIEW

1. REVIEW the Shabbat Seder up to this point. ASK the participants to list the various steps as you do them. PASS the *tzedakah* box for *Hakhanah L'Shabbat*, LIGHT the Shabbat candles (be sure to use fresh candles with new wicks) and CHANT the blessing, SING *Shalom Aleikhem*, PRACTICE the *Birkot ha-Mishpaḥah*, including the blessings for the children and the wife and husband, and CHANT the *Kiddush*.

2. EVALUATE where the people are having trouble. Once again, concentrate on the rituals learned at the last session. They will need the most review. REMIND the participants that to really get comfortable with the Hebrew they must practice at home with the tape. The more they practice, the easier it will get.

PART THREE—NETILAT YADAYIM

CONCEPTS

1. *Netilat Yadayim* means "washing the hands" but it is not an act of cleanliness. It is rather a ritual preparation for the meal. POINT OUT that *Netilat Yadayim* is not a special ritual for Shabbat only. ASK the participants if they know of another famous Jewish ceremony done in the home which contains *Netilat Yadayim*. THE ANSWER: the *Pesaḥ Seder*. REMIND them that just before the breaking of the *matzah*, the *Haggadah* stipulates that we wash our hands, reciting the exact same

blessing that we say for the washing at the Shabbat table.

2. EXPLAIN: The roots of *Netilat Yadayim* go back to the ancient Temple service. We have already heard one echo to the Temple service—the blessing of children using the Priestly Benediction. Here too we act as the Priests did in the Temple, ritually preparing ourselves for the meal to come, just as they would ritually cleanse their hands before performing the sacrifices.

TEACH the participants that Judaism was a Jerusalem Temple-centered religion until 70 C.E. when the Second Temple was destroyed. The destruction of the Temple meant the end of the animal sacrificial cult which had been the central feature of Jewish worship. Without a central Temple, local synagogues emerged where prayer and study took the place of animal sacrifices. The home ritual, too, became more important, and as a way to recall the Temple days, some of the religious behaviors contained echoes to the priests' actions around the altar. EMPHASIZE that the Rabbis likened the table to the altar in the Temple. Thus, some aspects of the rituals we do today also reflect those times.

OBJECTS

1. THE WASHING CUP AND BASIN. To engage in the ritual of *Netilat Yadayim*, you need a large washing cup or water pitcher. There are cups specifically designed for this purpose. Some of them are paired with a water basin in which to catch the water, although this is not necessary. The water can flow from the cup into the sink directly. The cup should be large enough to hold enough water to pour over the hands three times.

Any pitcher or glass will do, but ENCOURAGE participants to find the lovely brass washing cups and basins which are made in Israel specifically for this purpose. The cups in these sets have a pair of handles on either side to enable the person washing to hold the cup from either side. NOTE: It is not the little pitcher and basin often sold in synagogue gift stores. That is for *mayim aharonim*—the "after-waters," the Jewish version of a fingerbowl.

ASK those participants who may have brought such a washing set to class to share it with the group. Let them tell about it, where they found it, etc. If someone brought a *mayim aharonim* set, gently tell them it is to be used later in the Shabbat Seder, after the meal and just before *Birkat ha-Mazon*.

PRACTICE

1. TURN to the *Netilat Yadayim* blessing in the textbook. REMIND participants that they may follow with either the Hebrew and English columns or the transliteration and English columns.

2. READ and TRANSLATE the blessing for *Netilat Yadayim*.

Line 1 begins with the standard opening formula:

| *Barukh attah Adonai* | "Praised are You, Adonai." |

Line 2 continues the formula:

| *Eloheinu melekh ha-olam* | "Our God, Ruler of the universe." |

Line 3 continues with the formula which we learned in *Hadlakat Nerot*:

| *asher kidshanu b'mitzvotav* | "who has sanctified us through His commandments." |

Line 4 contains one word:

| *v'tzivanu* | "and commanded us," from the same root as *mitzvah*. |

Line 5 tells us what God has commanded us to do. In this case,

al	"concerning" or "on,"
netilat	"washing" (literally: "lifting up"),
yadayim	"hands."
	Together, "concerning the washing of hands."
	CONCENTRATE on each syllable as your review these unfamiliar words.

3. PRACTICE the entire blessing at least three times.

4. EXPLAIN that the Hebrew root of the word *netilat* is *natal* which can mean "to take" or "to lift up." We use this same word *netilat* when we "lift up" the *lulav* on *Sukkot*: the end of that blessing is " *al netilat lulav*."

ADD: One interpretation of the act of washing the hands is that we are "lifting up" the act of eating by ritually cleansing our hands. We are lifting ourselves above the animal level to the human level—the level of humankind created in God's image.

5. DEMONSTRATE how to wash hands. SET UP the wash cup and basin or go to a sink in the room. If necessary, you will need to fill a large pitcher with water from a drinking fountain from which you can refill the washing cup when necessary. BE SURE to have enough water for every person to wash. You do not want to lose the momentum of the moment by having to go fetch water.

EXPLAIN that before washing, it is traditional to take off all jewelry from the fingers. This is to make sure that nothing is between your body and the water. (The same requirement is made of people when they immerse themselves into the *mikvah*, the ritual bath.)

FILL the washing cup with water. PLACE IT in your right hand. POUR some water over the left hand, wetting it from the wrist down. TAKE the cup in your left hand and repeat for your right hand. (Actually, the order of hands is arbitrary.) YOU MAY repeat the entire procedure twice more for a total of three times. If you are at a sink, it is good etiquette to refill the washing cup for the next person. RECITE the blessing. DRY your hands with a towel. If necessary, RETURN to your seat and remain quiet until you recite the *ha-Motzi* and eat a piece of *ḥallah*.

ASK each participant to practice this procedure at least once. If you go to a sink, be sure to have a copy of the blessing nearby for the people to read. Or, you may want each person to practice the procedure and then say the blessing together. (It may be too threatening to ask people to read outloud the blessing they just learned by themselves.)

6. DISCUSS the "Practical Questions and Answers" concerning *Netilat Yadayim* listed in the textbook. SOLICIT questions about *Netilat Yadayim* and answer them.

PART FOUR—HA-MOTZI

CONCEPTS

1. EXPLAIN THAT *ḤALLAH* is A REMINDER OF MANNA. *Ḥallah* is the special white egg bread used for the Shabbat festive meal. Among its symbolic roots is the manna God provided to the Israelites during their forty years of wandering in the desert after the Exodus from Egypt. There are two *ḥallot* because in the biblical account, God provided a double portion of manna on Friday so the Israelites would not have to work to gather it on Shabbat. One explanation why we cover the *ḥallot* is to remind us of the dew which enveloped the manna in the desert, keeping it fresh.

2. EXPLAIN THAT *ḤALLAH* is A REMINDER OF THE SHEWBREADS. In the Temple in Jerusalem, each of the twelve tribes weekly brought a loaf of braided bread which was kept on a special gold table. These were called the Shew bread. The braiding on the *ḥallah* reminds us of the unity of all Israel.

3. EXPLAIN THAT *ḤALLAH* is A REMINDER OF THE MITZVAH OF *ḤALLAH*. In Numbers 15.19-20, a commandment was given to set aside a portion of any dough for the Temple priests. This was a tithe, a kind of biblical tax. When the Temple was destroyed, the priests no longer received their portion, but the practice of taking a portion of the dough (and now burning it in the oven) has continued. *Ḥallah* is still made by fulfilling this *mitzvah*.

OBJECTS

1. *ḤALLAH*. The *ḥallah* bread is usually made of white flour mixed with eggs to give it a slightly yellow tinge. The word *ḥallah* actually means "cake" or "loaf." Historically, white bread was a special delicacy saved for the Shabbat table. During the week, most people (particularly in Eastern Europe) ate dark bread.

POINT OUT that two complete *ḥallot* are required for the Shabbat dinner table, representing the double portion of manna. NOTE that the *ḥallot* are usually braided, although this is not a requirement. Jewish bakers through the ages have enjoyed creating a variety of *ḥallah* shapes. BRING Volume VI, PAGE 1419 of the *Encyclopedia Judaica* published by Keter Press. SHOW the participants the different *ḥallah* shapes pictured.

2. *ḤALLAH* COVER. The *ḥallot* are covered by a special cloth when they are on the Shabbat table. TELL the participants that any white cloth will do, but ENCOURAGE them to acquire or make a decorative *ḥallah* cover to embellish this part of the Shabbat Seder. EXPLAIN the reasons given for the *ḥallot* being covered: (1) as a reminder of the dew on the manna, (2) to save the *ḥallot* from "embarrassment" when precedence is given to the wine.

3. *ḤALLAH* PLATE. The *ḥallot* can be placed directly on the table, although many families acquire a *ḥallah* plate which usually contains a wooden cutting board. Sometimes the silver plate which holds the cutting board is quite ornate with slogans such as *L'khvod Shabbat v'Yom Tov*—"In honor of Shabbat and holidays" or it may have the *ha-Motzi* blessing

engraved around the edges.

4. *HALLAH* KNIFE. For those who like to slice the *hallah*, decorative silver or brass knives are available for the task. These too usually have engraved upon them a slogan such as those found on the *hallah* plates and covers.

5. SALT SHAKER. POINT OUT that the ritual in its most traditional form requires the sprinkling of salt on the *hallah*. Most families use any available salt shaker for this purpose.

PRACTICE

1. TURN to the *ha-Motzi* in the textbook. REMIND participants that they may follow in the Hebrew and English columns or in the transliteration and English columns.

2. BEGIN the translation of the *ha-Motzi*.

Line 1 begins with the standard formula:

Barukh attah Adonai	"Praised are You, Adonai."

Line 2 continues:

Eloheinu melekh ha-olam	"Our God, Ruler of the universe."

Line 3 contains the specific words for the breaking of bread:

ha-Motzi	"who brings forth," from the Hebrew word *yatzah*—"to bring out/forth,"
lehem	"bread,"
min	"from,"
ha-aretz	"the earth."

NOTE that the word *lehem*—"bread" is used and not the word *hallah*. *Ha-Motzi* can be made over any bread made of the five grains indigenous to the land of Israel: wheat, barley, spelt, oats, rye. *Hallah* is the special bread used at the Shabbat table made from one of these types of grain.

3. TEACH the tune for *ha-Motzi*. REPEAT at least twice until the participants seem to grasp the melody. Some may want to sing "Amen" at the end of the blessing. REMIND them that saying "Amen" is redundant if you yourself are reciting the blessing. "Amen" means "so be it," and developed to allow those who could not say blessings to participate in them. Since we are learning to recite the blessings personally, we need not say "Amen" at the end of any of the blessings in the Shabbat Seder (with the exception of one blessing in the *Birkat ha-Mazon* which is a special case).

4. DEMONSTRATE the proper procedure for breaking *hallah*. RECALL that the *Netilat Yadayim* is immediately prerequisite to the *ha-Motzi* and is, in fact, considered one act with the breaking of bread. Therefore, there is no talking between the time one finishes saying *Netilat Yadayim* and the recitation of the *ha-Motzi* and the eating of the *hallah*.

As soon as everyone has finished washing and reciting *Netilat Yadayim*, someone preselected for the job should REMOVE the *hallah* cover. Then, the leader PLACES one *hallah* on top of the other, and NICKS the end of the top *hallah* with a knife to mark the piece to be broken off for the blessing (optional). Then, either the leader or someone who is preassigned the role or everyone together CHANTS the *ha-Motzi* blessing. The end piece of the *hallah* is torn off, salt is SPRINKLED on it, it is BROKEN (or sliced) into as many pieces as there are people at the table, placed on another plate and PASSED around the table for everyone to take and eat. At that point, people are again free to talk.

5. PRACTICE the *ha-Motzi* ritual with the group.

6. As you enjoy eating the *hallah*, DISCUSS the "Practical Questions and Answers" about *hallah* and the bread-breaking ritual. TAKE A POLL among the group as to "slicers," "the tearers," and the "pullers." COMMENT on those families with young children who hate crusts. We call them "the cavers," experts at mining the innards of *hallot*.

7. If you have determined that there is enough time in the course, ANNOUNCE that the group will learn how to bake *hallah* during one of the class sessions to come. If you do not know how to bake *hallah* yourself, ASK around the synagogue for someone who can teach the group how to do it. It is great fun for the people to learn. If there is not enough time in the course, REFER the participants to the "no-fail" *hallah* recipe in the "Shabbat Gallery" chapter of the text.

PART FIVE—THE SHABBAT SEUDAH

CONCEPTS

1. *SEUDAT MITZVAH*. TEACH that Shabbat dinner is a *seudat mitzvah*—"a commanded meal." This connotes a festive meal, complete with a special dinner and special activities. EXPLAIN that there are many kinds of *seudot mitzvah*, times when we are commanded to eat a meal. For example, the mourners must eat after a funeral in recognition that, even in the face of death, life must go on. The Friday night meal is one of three commanded meals of Shabbat. DESCRIBE the other two: Shabbat lunch and *Seudah Sh'lishit*, the third meal in the afternoon between *Minḥa* and *Ma'ariv*. (If someone asks about Shabbat breakfast, EXPLAIN that it is not considered a formal meal.)

2. A CIVILIZED EATING EXPERIENCE. Unlike most of the meals we eat in a week, the Shabbat dinner experience should be relaxed and civilized. POINT OUT that family members are usually dressed a little nicer than usual, many families eat in the formal dining room instead of the kitchen or breakfast area, and a beautiful table is set. Moreover, favorite foods are usually on the menu and often several courses are served as opposed to the family-style mode of eating common to the weekday. Table talk centers on significant topics rather than the gossip of the workplace. The hurried ten minute gulped down dinner is lengthened to a leisurely pace which can stretch over several hours.

OBJECTS

POINT OUT that there are no specific objects for the meal except favorite foods. There certainly are traditional Shabbat delicacies such as chicken soup, gefilte fish, and any number of baked chicken dishes. But in some families, more modern foods find their way onto the Shabbat menu. Some families even vary the dishes depending on who eats what. SHARE the "Recipe" section in the "Shabbat Gallery" chapter of the text with the group.

PRACTICE

DESCRIBE the meal as both leisurely and well-paced. Often, there are several courses to be served: soup, fish and the main meal. Some families assign roles to the children to help with the serving.

Some families engage in formal study at the Shabbat table. One family we interviewed developed a very ambitious program of preparing commentaries on the weekly Torah portion. There are a number of texts available for those families who may want to engage in this kind of Shabbat study. They are listed in the "Selected Bibliography" in the text.

SUGGEST that whatever the ages of the children in the family, it is possible to have Family Sharing at the dinner table. In the text, we suggest asking a simple question: "What was your favorite time this week?" In our home, the oldest child has the responsibility for asking this question for everyone around the table. When everyone has had a turn answering, the entire group turns to her and asks: "Havi, what was your favorite time this week?" and she gets the honor of being last.

For families with young children, REFER them to the chapter entitled "The Shabbat Gallery." Here we have collected a variety of pre-Shabbat and Shabbat table activities to keep the little ones involved.

DISCUSS how difficult it is for young children to sit at the table all the way through the meal. While adults relish the idea of leisurely sitting around the table, children are usually "antsy" by the time the main meal is over. Most families we spoke to allow the children to leave the table to play until it is time for *Birkat ha-Mazon* when they are called back to the table. Usually, this practice works.

Of course, *Z'mirot* are an essential part of the *Shabbat Seudah*. But they deserve their own chapter!

ASSIGNMENT

1. ASK participants to bring all of their Shabbat ritual objects for the next session. This will be a culminating Shabbat Seder together, reviewing all parts of the ritual. They should bring: *tzedakah* money, candlesticks and candles, and a *Kiddush* cup. You will provide the washing cup and basin, towel and *ḥallah* materials.
2. If the next session is your last class together, ASSIGN individuals responsiblity to bring items for a pot-luck Shabbat dinner. If your synagogue policy allows, you could even bring in Kosher food for a real meal. If not, create a mock meal with cakes and cookies, etc. Let everyone pitch in by assigning someone to buy or make the *ḥallot*, bring the wine, buy some flowers, and provide the other goodies. Be sure everyone has the responsibility to bring something.
3. REMIND the participants to celebrate the coming Shabbat in as full a manner as comfortable. ENCOURAGE them to practice the Hebrew blessings using the tape.

Session 6 Outline

OVERVIEW:

In this session, participants will learn (1) how to sing *Z'mirot*, (2) the meaning and procedure for reciting *Birkat ha-Mazon*, and will (3) conclude the course with a complete run-through of the Shabbat Seder.

BACKGROUND:

The singing of *Z'mirot*—"songs"—is a traditional part of the Shabbat Seder celebration. It is rooted in the concept of *Oneg Shabbat*—"the joy of Shabbat." Singing is one of the most enjoyable activities to do around the table and the poets and song-writers throughout Jewish history have provided us with a wealth of material from which to choose.

The *Birkat ha-Mazon*, the blessings after the food, is commanded in the Bible: *v'akhalta v'savata u'vayrakhta et Adonai Elokhekhah*—"you shall eat and be satisfied and you shall bless *Adonai*, Your God" (Deuteronomy 8:10). Unlike some other religions which prescribe Grace before eating, Judaism tells us to thank God after we are satisfied so we will not become callous to the bounty which God affords us. The *Birkat ha-Mazon* is our vehicle for the expression of the many thanks we offer after enjoying any meal.

GOALS:

1. Participants will review the Shabbat Seder ritual by re-creating it in class.

2. Participants will learn to sing at least two Shabbat *Z'mirot*.

3. Participants will learn the meaning of the major parts of the *Birkat ha-Mazon* (the "short" form) and how to chant them.

4. Participants will summarize their feelings about the impact of the course on themselves and their families.

PREPARATION:

If you have decided that this is to be your last class session, you should assign participants various items to bring to re-create the Shabbat Seder in the class. Unlike the first Shabbat Seder demonstration that you set up yourself, your group should help you considerably in acquiring the necessary items for this culminating activity.

By and large, you can trust people to remember to bring the items they volunteered to get. However, to be safe, you may want to call each person with a reminder of what they agreed to bring. Or, you bring the basic things: candles, wine and *hallah*, just in case someone forgets something.

You should set up the entire Shabbat table as you did for the first class session demonstration. You'll need:

White tablecloth	Flowers (NOT optional this time—be festive!)
Tzedakah box	Candlesticks
Candles and matches	Kiddush cup
Kipot	*Washing cup, basin and towel*
Wine	*Hallah* plate, cover and knife
2 *Hallot*	Plates, cups, napkins, etc.
Salt shaker	

You may also want to bring some supplementary resource material on Shabbat observance from the synagogue library for those who want to continue to read and study about Shabbat.

PART ONE—SHARING

1. WELCOME. At this session, everyone will arrive with hands full of their ritual items and assigned goodies. The room should be bustling with activity, everyone joining in the preparation of the table. This is a great opportunity to REINFORCE the importance of *Hakhanah L'Shabbat*.

2. SHARING. Once again, ALLOW about ten minutes for participants to share what has been happening in their own homes on Friday night. You may get some testimonials about how much they have learned and incorporated into their home celebrations. Thank them and continue to the Shabbat Seder review.

PART TWO—REVIEW

1. At this session, you will have a complete run-through of the Shabbat Seder up to the singing of *Z'mirot*. This review should

be conducted in a manner similar to the original Shabbat Seder demonstration you gave at the first session. The only difference here is that you should not lead it! While it may seem remarkable, the participants themselves should be able to lead the group through the Shabbat Seder. You can begin by suggesting they turn to the first chapter which contains the Shabbat Seder guide, and they may occasionally need prompting, but now you should sit back and watch them as they perform the rituals they have worked so hard to learn. PARTICIPATE, but DO NOT DOMINATE!

2. When you have completed the ritual up to the point of the meal, CONGRATULATE the participants on a job well done! Then, INVITE them to partake of the goodies while you turn to the chapter on *Z'mirot*.

PART THREE—Z'MIROT

CONCEPTS

1. *ONEG SHABBAT.* It should be easy to discuss the concept of *Oneg Shabbat* at this session since most of the participants will feel happy that they have learned so much in the class. *Oneg Shabbat* means "the joy of Shabbat." EMPHASIZE that an important part of the meal is the singing of these special Shabbat songs.

OBJECTS

1. Collections of *Z'mirot* called "*benschers*" in Yiddish are often found in homes where Shabbat is celebrated. These booklets usually contain the words to the most traditional of Shabbat *Z'mirot*, the *Birkat ha-Mazon* and sometimes the Jewish wedding service or Shabbat Seder blessings. Often times, these booklets are given out at Bar/Bat Mitzvahs and weddings to be used by guests at the celebration dinner. If you can, BRING some "*benschers*" with you to class to show the people.

POINT OUT that many families collect these booklets which usually have the name of the honoree and the date of the event. Although many such booklets are not uniform in pagination which makes it difficult to use at the table for communal singing, having these souvenirs is another valued part of a family's ritual items.

PRACTICE

1. TURN to the *Z'mirot* section of the textbook. Several *Z'mirot* are found there. PICK OUT one or two to teach the group. START with "*Shabbat Shalom*," (a.k.a. *Bim Bam*) which many of the participants may know. TRY "*Hiney Ma Tov u'Ma Nayim*," another familiar song. If they are a particularly capable group, teach "*Tzur Mishelo.*" As with the blessings, TRANSLATE the Hebrew for them line-by-line; then TEACH THE TUNE line-by-line. PRACTICE the songs until most of the people seem comfortable with them. REMIND the people that several of the *Z'mirot* are sung on the audiotape.

2. DESCRIBE the practice in some families to go around the table and ask each person to pick a favorite *Zemer* for singing. This can be fun and ensure that at least a few songs will be sung.

3. ANOTHER POINT is to be made for families with small children. It is unusual but perfectly permissible to sing *Z'mirot* before the bulk of the Shabbat Seder blessings are recited. One family we interviewed sings for at least 5—10 minutes after candlelighting and before blessing the children. They begin with *Shalom Aleikhem* and keep on singing. They report that it is very difficult to get the children to participate in a lot of singing after the major part of the meal is completed, so they have adopted this strategy. Another family reported that sometimes they recite the *Birkat ha-Mazon* immediately after dessert and save the singing of *Z'mirot* till later so that the children can run off if they wish. These are all practical suggestions that help people paint their own picture of the Shabbat Seder.

4. REVIEW the other "Practical Questions and Answers" about *Z'mirot*.

PART FOUR—BIRKAT HA-MAZON

CONCEPTS

1. BLESSINGS AFTER THE MEAL. ASK this question: "Why do we say *Birkat ha-Mazon* after dinner? Shouldn't we thank God before we eat?" DISCUSS this issue with the group. POINT OUT that it was extremely important to the Rabbis that we not forget who is the Ultimate Source of sustenance.

2. FOUR THEMES OF THE *BIRKAT HA-MAZON.* BEFORE translating the blessings of the *Birkat ha-Mazon*, lead the participants through an outline of the major themes to help them organize the information.

DESCRIBE the four themes of the *Birkat ha-Mazon*:

a) *Blessing for Food.* TURN to the blessing which ends *ḥazan et ha-kol.* POINT OUT that in Jewish liturgy, the last line usually summarizes the theme of the prayer. ASK someone to read the last line, line 14, in the Hebrew and English. EMPHASIZE the universalistic notion that God provides food for all the people and creatures God created.

b)   *Blessing for the Land.* TURN to the blessing which ends *al ha-aretz v'al ha-mazon.* ASK someone to read the last line of this blessing, lines 5 and 6.

   ASK: "What land do you think the prayer is referring to?" In the context of this prayer, there can only be one land—the land of Israel. DISCUSS the progression of first blessing God who has universalistic concerns and then blessing God who has a special relationship with this people to whom He has given the "good land" of *Eretz Yisrael.*

c)   *Blessing for Jerusalem.* TURN to the third major blessing in the *Birkat ha-Mazon* which ends *boney v'rahamav Yerushalayim, Amen.* ASK someone to read the Hebrew and English of lines 9 and 10. TELL the participants that originally this prayer contained thanks for Jerusalem and the Temple, but after the destruction of the Temple, the wording was changed to emphasize the Messianic vision of rebuilding the holy city.

d)   *Blessing of Goodness.* TURN to the fourth major blessing which begins *Barukh attah Adonai Eloheinu melekh ha-olam ha-tov v'ha-mativ lakol.*

   EXPLAIN: This blessing was added to the three biblically commanded prayers by the Rabbinic sages soon after the destruction of the Second Temple. ASK someone to read it in Hebrew and English. DISCUSS the importance of this prayer in the context of history. EMPHASIZE that even in the face of adversity, the Rabbis asserted God's goodness.

   TELL the participants that, although there are other themes sounded in the rest of the prayers which make up the *Birkat ha-Mazon,* these four major themes are the most important.

OBJECTS

The only object needed for *Birkat ha-Mazon* is a book with the texts of the blessings. REMIND the participants that books which contain the *Birkat ha-Mazon* and *Z'mirot* are called "*benschers.*" "*Bensch*" in Yiddish means "bless," so "*benschers*" are "blessing books." In Yiddish, *Birkat ha-Mazon* is known as "the bensching,"—"the blessing." Some people may recall parents or grandparents who would "*bensch likht.*" This meant "bless the lights," meaning the candles. Both the short and complete version of the *Birkat ha-Mazon* are found in the textbook.

OPTIONAL: Some families have little sets which contain a miniature water pitcher and basin. This is used for *mayim aharonim*—"the after-waters," the Jewish version of fingerbowls. The set is passed around immediately prior to *Birkat ha-Mazon* for participants to wet their fingers, symbolically ending the meal. There is no specific blessing for this custom. If someone has a *mayim aharonim* set or if you can find one, show it to the group. DIFFERENTIATE between this and the objects necessary for *Netilat Yadayim.*

PRACTICE

MAKE IT CLEAR that *Birkat ha-Mazon* is recited after every meal in which bread is eaten. Naturally, the *Birkat ha-Mazon* for Shabbat has additional prayers in honor of the special day.

DECISION POINT: Depending on the objectives you set out for the course, you will have time to teach either the short version or the complete *Birkat ha-Mazon.* To teach the complete *Birkat ha-Mazon,* you will need to devote at least an entire 1 and 1/2 hour session. We have included the complete *Birkat ha-Mazon* in the text. Our experience tells us that you will more likely opt to teach the short version of the *Birkat ha-Mazon* to the class, especially if many of the participants are just beginning their Shabbat observance. Thus, we will present a teaching outline limited to the short version.

NOTE: The short version text is the one which was adopted by the major arms of the Conservative Movement in 1977. It contains a few more verses than the widely popular version used in synagogues for many years prior to that date. Actually, it is a more representative "short" version since it includes all four of the major themes. As always, you have choices to make as a teacher as to what will work best in your own local situation.

1.   TURN to the *Birkat ha-Mazon* in the textbook. BEGIN with *Shir ha-Ma'alot,* "a song of the ascent," Psalm 126. The "ascent" refers to the hoped-for return of the exiles to Zion in the days of the Messiah. POINT OUT that since Shabbat is considered a foretaste of the world-to-come, this introductory Psalm sets the mood for thanking God for the food we have just eaten. In addition, REFER to the obligation recorded in *Pirke Avot,* the Ethics of the Fathers, (3:4), cited in the textbook, which states that if three people have eaten at a table and words of Torah are spoken, it is as though they had eaten at the Lord's table. Since this biblical paragraph qualifies as "words of Torah," reciting *Shir ha-Ma'alot* fulfills this suggestion.

   TRANSLATE the text. Practice the Hebrew words of each line, repeating from the beginning occasionally.

Line 1 gives the title of the Psalm

Shir   "a song,"

ba-Ma'alot	"of ascents" (literally: "the heights.")

Line 2

b'shuv Adonai	"when Adonai restores" (*shuv* means returns)
et shivat tzion	"(for) the fortunes of Zion."(Literally "returns the returning to Zion")

Line 3

hayinu	"we will be,"
k'holmim	*k* means "as" and *holmim* means "dreamers."

Together, lines 2 and 3 are: "When Adonai restores the fortunes of Zion, we will be as in a dream."

Line 4

az	meaning "then."
yimaley	is the word for "will be filled."
s'hok	means "laughter,"
pinu	"our mouths."

Line 5

ul'shoneinu	is a combination of terms - *u* stands for "and," *l'shonei* means "tongues," and the *nu* ending means "our."
rina	is a word for "song."

Together, lines 4 and 5 translated are: "Then our mouths will be filled with laughter and our tongues (filled with) songs of joy."

Line 6 tells of what will happen when the other peoples hear of this happening.

az	means "then," the same word as in line 4.
yomru	means "they will say,"
va'goyim	translates as "among the nations."

Line 7

higdil	means "great (things)," from the same root as *gadol* "great."
Adonai	is a name of God.
la'asot	is a word meaning "to do" and
im elleh	is a term meaning "for these," referring to the Israelites.

Together, lines 6 and 7 are: "Then they will say among the nations: 'Adonai did great things for them.'"

Now the Psalmist asserts that, indeed, God will do great things for us.

Line 8

higdil Adonai la'asot	"Adonai will do great things"
imanu	"for us."

Line 9

hayinu	"we will be"
s'mehim	"happy."

The Psalmist begins to direct the prayer directly to God. **Line 10:**

Shuva	"restore,"
Adonai	"Lord,"
et-sh'vitenu	"our fortune."

Line 11 continues the thought:

ka'afikim	"like streams,"
ba'negev	"in the Negev."

Line 12 brings home the moral of the story.

ha'zorim	"those who sow,"
b'dima	"in tears,"

Line 13

b'rina	"with songs,"
yiktzoru	"they shall reap."

Line 14

halokh yelekh	is a term meaning "he who walks along."
uvakho	means "and weeps,"—

Line 15

nosei	"carrying,"
meshekh ha-zara	"his sack of seeds."

Line 16

bo-yavo	"He will come back,"
v'rina	"*with* song,"

Line 17

nosei	"carrying,"
alumotav	"his sheaves."

Together, lines 14-17: "He who walks along and weeps, carrying his sack of seeds—He will come back with song, carrying his sheaves."

REVIEW the meaning of the Psalm in English. REPEAT the entire Psalm in Hebrew once for practice. TEACH the tune to *Shir ha-Ma'alot* line by line until all have learned the tune.

2. EXPLAIN AND TRANSLATE THE "INVITATION TO RECITE GRACE." Judaism uses a language of communal prayer. Thus, when three or more adults eat together, they join in the *Zimmun*—literally "invitation" . This is done by assigning one person to lead the short responsive section before the *Ḥazan et ha-kol* paragraph. NOTE that the first word in the *Zimmun* is *Rabotai*—literally "gentlemen." Some translate *Rabotai* as "friends." Others handle what seems to be a slight to the women at the table by either adding the word *u'gevirotai*—"and ladies," or by changing *Rabotai* to *haverai*—a better word for "friends." You will need to decide which formulation is appropriate in your setting. NOTE also that when ten or more adults eat together, the term *Eloheinu* is added at two places in the *Zimmun*. Since ten is the required minimum for a *minyan*—"a quorum," it is considered proper to include this extra reference to God—a greater *mitzvah* which encourages greater community.

TURN to the *Zimmun* and begin the translation. The designated leader begins:

Ḥaverai n'varekh	"my friends let us praise (or "give thanks"). Participants should recognize the root of *nevarekh* as realted to *barukh*—"bless" or "praise". PRACTICE the Hebrew at least twice.

In line 2, those at the table respond with:

Yehi	"May,"

—44—

shem	"name,"
Adonai	a word for God,
m'vorakh	"be blessed,"
mei'attah	"from now,"
v'ad olam	"and until forever."

Together, the line translates: "May Adonai's name be blessed now and forever." PRACTICE the Hebrew once.

In line 3, the leader repeats this line:

Yehi shem Adonai m'vorakh mei'attah v'ad olam

Line 4. The leader then says:

Bir'shut	"with the consent (or "permission"),"
ḥaverai	"(of) my friends." POINT OUT that whichever term is used for "friends," be consistent in lines 1 and 4.
nevarekh	"let us praise,"
(Eloheinu)	("our God"),
she'akhalnu mishelo	"for we have eaten of His (food),"

Together: "Let us praise (our God) the One whose food we have eaten." The Hebrew of this line assumes the words "the One" (if Eloheinu is not said) and "food" which is implied in the word *she'akhalnu*. PRACTICE the Hebrew at least twice.

The response from those assembled is on lines 6 and 7.

Barukh	"praised,"
(Eloheinu)	("our God"),
she'akhalnu mishelo	"of whose (food) we have eaten,"

Line 7

| *uv'tuvo* | "and by whose goodness" (from the word *tov*—"good"), |
| *ḥayinu* | "we live" (related to the word *ḥai'yim*—"life.") |

Together lines 6 and 7 translate: "Praised be (our God) the One of whose food we have eaten and by whose goodness we live." PRACTICE the Hebrew.

On lines 8 and 9, the leader repeats the exact same formula as the others just recited on lines 6 and 7.

The *Zimmun* ends with **line 10**, in unison:

Barukh	"Praised,"
hu	"(be) He,"
u'varukh	"and praised be,"
sh'mo	"His name."

Together: "Praised be He and praised be His name." POINT OUT that this line is the same line said in response to the formula "*Barukh attah Adonai*" in the prayer services by a person leading the congregation. PRACTICE the Hebrew.

REVIEW the Hebrew of the entire *Zimmun* at least once. TEACH the tunes to the *Zimmun* line-by-line.

3. TURN to the Blessing for Food: *Hazan et ha-kol*. TRANSLATE line 1 which should look very familiar to your group by now:

Barukh attah Adonai

Eloheinu melekh ha-olam   Means "Praised are You, Adonai, Our God, Ruler of the universe."

Line 2 sets the theme:

hazan	"who feeds," (related to the word *mazon*, as in *Birkat ha-Mazon*),
et ha'olam	"the world (or "universe")."

Line 3 continues the thought:

kulo	"all of it,"
b'tuvo	"with His goodness" (from the word *tov*—"good").

Line 4 concludes:

b'ḥeyn	"with graciousness"
b'ḥesed	"with love," (literally "with mercy"),
u-v'raḥamim	"and with compassion."

Together, lines 1-4: "Praised are You, *Adonai*, Our God, Ruler of the universe, who feeds the whole world through His goodness, with graciousness, love and with compassion." PRACTICE the Hebrew.

Line 5 continues the theme:

Hu	"He"
noten	"provides" (literally "gives"),
leḥem	"food" (literally "bread," as in *ha-Motzi leḥem min ha-aretz*),
l'khol	"to every,"
basar	"creature" (literally—"flesh");

Line 6

ki	"because,"
l'olam	"is forever,"
ḥasdo	"His love."

Together, lines 5 and 6: "He provides food to every creature because His love (endures) forever." PRACTICE the Hebrew.

The next lines infer a hope that God will never allow us to go hungry.

Line 7

U-v'tuvo ha-gadol	"and through His great (*gadol*) goodness (*tuvo*),"
tamid lo	a combination of words meaning "never" (*tamid* literally means "always" but *lo* is a negative "no"—together you get "never"),
ḥasar	"failed,"
lanu	"us."

Together: "And through His great goodness has never failed us." PRACTICE the Hebrew.

Line 8

V'al yeḥ'sar lanu	"and will never fail," (a combination of the terms *v'*—"and," *al*—"never," *yeḥsar*—"fail"),
mazon	"food" (as in *Birkat ha-Mazon*),
l'olam va'ed	"forever."

Although a bit convoluted in the Hebrew, the meaning of this sentence is: "And food will not fail us ever." PRACTICE the Hebrew.

Line 9 finishes the thought:

ba'avur	"for the sake,"
sh'mo	"His name,"
ha-gadol	"great."

Line 10:

ki	"because,"
hu	"He,"
El	a name of God,
zan	"feeds,"
u-m'farnes	(a hard "s" sound at the end of this word)—"and provides,"
la-kol	"for all."
	·PRACTICE the Hebrew of lines 9-10.

Line 11

u-metiv	"and is good," (from the word *tov*—"good"),
la-kol	"to all."

Line 12

u-mekhin	"and prepares,"
mazon	"food,"
l'khol	"for all,"
b'riyotav	"His creatures,"

Line 13

asher	"which,"
bara	"He created."
	PRACTICE the Hebrew of lines 11-13.

The prayer ends with the thematic statement:

Line 14

Barukh	"Praised,"
attah	"are You,"
Adonai	a name of God,
hazan	"Provider,"
et ha-kol	"for all."
	PRACTICE the Hebrew of line 14.

REREAD the English of the paragraph. ASK participants to find the words that are repeated several times. They are: variations of the word *tov*—"good," the word *kol*—"all," and variations of *mazon*—"food, provide, feed." So, the message is that God provides food for every creature through His goodness.

PRACTICE the Hebrew of this paragraph at least once all the way through. TEACH the tune to this paragraph. Many will be familiar with it. GO SLOWLY to make sure people practice the correct Hebrew pronunciations.

4. TURN to the Blessing for the Land: *al ha-aretz v'al ha-mazon.*

Line 1

Nodeh lekha	"we thank You."
Adonai Eloheinu	"Adonai, Our God."

PRACTICE the Hebrew at least once. (By the way, this material will probably be unfamiliar to many participants. It was added to the official "short version" of the *Birkat ha-Mazon* adopted by all branches of the Conservative Movement in 1977.)

Line 2

al	"for,"
she'hinhalta	"You have given as an inheritance" (this is a form of the word we learned twice in the *Kiddush*— *hinhilanu* and *hinhaltanu*),
la'avoteinu	"to our ancestors."

Together lines 1 and 2 mean: "We thank you, Adonai Our God for Your inheritance to our ancestors." PRACTICE the Hebrew.

Line 3

eretz	"a land,"
hemdah	"desirable,"
tovah	"good,"
ur'havah	"and spacious."

Line 4 continues to list the "inheritance:"

b'rit	"the covenant" (between God and the Jewish people),
v'Torah	"and the Torah,"
hayim	"life,"
u'mazon	"and food."

PRACTICE the Hebrew of lines 3 and 4.

Line 5 turns to praising God:

Yitbarakh shimkha	"may Your name (*shimkha*) be praised (*yitbarakh*)."

Line 6

b'fi	"by the mouth of"
khol hai	"every living thing,"
tamid	"always,"
l'olam va'ed	"forever."

Together, lines 5 and 6: "May Your name be praised by the mouth of every living thing." PRACTICE the Hebrew of lines 5 and 6.

Line 7 brings the proof text from the Bible (Deut. 8.10):

Kakatuv:	"as it is written."

Line 8 begins the quotation:

v'akhalta	"and (when) you have eaten,"
v'savata	"and are satisfied."

Line 9 tells what to do next:

u'veyrakhta	"(and) you shall praise (compare *barukh*),"

Line 10

al ha-aretz ha-tovah	"for the good land" (the Hebrew puts the noun before the adjective),
asher	"which,"
natan	"He gave,"
lakh	"to you."

Together, lines 7-10: "As it is written: 'And when you have eaten and are satisfied, you shall praise Adonai, Your God for the good land which He gave to you.'" PRACTICE the Hebrew.

Line 11-12 summarizes the theme of the prayer. **Line 11:**

Barukh attah Adonai	"Praised are You, Adonai,"

Line 12

al ha-aretz	"for the land,"
ve'al ha-mazon	"and for the sustenance (literally 'food')." PRACTICE the Hebrew of lines 11 and 12 at least twice.

REVIEW the Hebrew once from lines 1—12. TEACH the tune line by line.

5. TURN to the Blessing for Jerusalem. **Line 1** states the theme:

Uv'ney Yerushalayim	"rebuild Jerusalem,"—

Line 2

ir	"the city,"
ha-kodesh	"the holy,"
bim'herah	"soon" (literally "quickly"),
v'yamenu	"in our days" (plural of *yom*—"day").

Together lines 1 and 2: "Rebuild Jerusalem Your holy city, soon, in our days." PRACTICE the Hebrew.

Line 3 and 4 summarize the theme of the prayer:

Barukh attah Adonai	"Praised are You, Adonai,"

Line 4

boneh	"who rebuilds,"
v'rahamav	"in His compassion,"
Yerushalayim	"Jerusalem,"
amen	"Amen."

EMPHASIZE that this third blessing for Jerusalem also implies a hope for the Messianic Age. Participants may ask why we say "Amen" at the end of this blessing when earlier we learned that one need not say "Amen" after reciting a blessing oneself. The answer is that this blessing for Jerusalem completes the three biblically commanded blessings in the *Birkat ha-Mazon*. Even though the Rabbis added the prayers we will turn to next, this marked the end of the *Birkat ha-Mazon* at one time. If someone asks why we say "*v'imru Amen*," or "*v'nomar Amen*" at the end of some prayers, EXPLAIN that the words *v'imru* and *v'nomar* mean "and let us say," asking those who are participating to acknowledge the just-recited blessing with "Amen."

6. TURN to the Blessing of Goodness.

Lines 1 and 2 begin with the standard blessing formula:

Barukh attah, Adonai,	
Eloheinu melekh	
ha-olam	"Praised are You, Adonai, Our God, Ruler of the universe."

Line 3 states the theme:

ha-melekh	"the Ruler,"
ha-tov	"(the) good,"
v'ha-mativ	"and does good,"
la-kol	"to all."

Together, line 3 reads: "The Ruler who is good and does good to all." PRACTICE the Hebrew.

Line 4

Hu hetiv	"He has been good,"
hu metiv	"He is good,"

Line 5

hu yetiv lanu	"He will be good to us." This poetic use of the past, present and future tenses of the word for "good" serves to emphasize the theme of God's goodness. PRACTICE the Hebrew.

The use of three tenses for emphasis continues in **line 6**:

hu gemalanu	"He bestowed upon us,"
hu gomlenu	"He bestows upon us,"

Line 7

hu yigmilenu	"He will bestow upon us,"
la'ad	"forever"
	PRACTICE the Hebrew.

Line 8

hen	"grace,"
vahesed	"and kindness,"
verahamim	"and compassion"—that's what God bestows upon us.

Line 9

vizakenu	"and gain for us,"
limot	"the days of,"
ha-mashiah	"the Messiah."

REVIEW the meaning of the Blessing of Goodness. PRACTICE the Hebrew. TEACH the tune, line-by-line.

7. TURN to the Blessing for Shabbat. (There are three other "*Harahaman*" prayers in the 1977 short version of the *Birkat ha-Mazon*: for the land of residence, for Jews who suffer and for the State of Israel. They can be found in the long version of the *Birkat ha-Mazon* in the textbook should you wish to teach them at this point. Our experience is that there is not enough time to teach these if you are only teaching the "short version.") The "*Harahaman*" prayer for Shabbat begins on **line 1**:

Harahaman hu	"(May) the Compassionate One (He),"
yanhileynu	"give us as an inheritance," (another form of the word *hinhilanu* and *hinhaltanu* we learned in the *Kiddush*).

Line 2

yom	"a day,"
she'kulo	"that is completely,"
Shabbat	"Shabbat,"

u'menuḥa	"and rest."

Line 3

l'ḥayei ha-olamim	"in life everlasting" "in the world to come."
	PRACTICE the Hebrew.

POINT OUT that this prayer is reminiscent of the Rabbinic view that the Shabbat is a foretaste of the world to come in the Messianic Age. TEACH the tune, line-by-line.

8. TURN to *Venisa verakha*—the last prayer in the "short" version of the *Birkat ha-Mazon*. NOTE: this version of the short *Birkat ha-Mazon* has combined a verse from the sections of the complete *Birkat ha-Mazon* which begin *Bamarov ye-lamdu* and *Migdol yeshuot*. Some of the participants will be used to beginning this section with *Migdol yeshuot*. Should you wish to do so, TURN to the section with the complete *Birkat ha-Mazon* in the textbook.

Translate beginning with **line 1**:

Venisa	"Then shall we receive,"
verakha	"blessing,"
ma'ayt	"from,"
Adonai	a name of God.

Line 2

utzedakah	"and justice,"
may'Elohei	"from the God,"
yishenu	"of our deliverance."

Line 3

venimtza	"and (may) we find,"
ḥen	"favor,"
vesekhel	"understanding,"
tov	"good,"

Line 4

b'einei	"in the eyes of,"
Elohim	a name of God,
v'adam	"and people."
	PRACTICE the Hebrew.

Together, lines 3 and 4: "and may we find favor and good understanding in the eyes of God and people."

Line 5 begins one of the most famous lines in Jewish liturgy which, significantly, concludes the *Birkat ha-Mazon*:

Oseh shalom bimromov	"He who makes peace in His heavens"
hu ya'aseh	"(May) He make"
shalom alenu	"peace for us"
v'al kol Yisrael	"and for all Israel"
v'imru Amen	"and let us say: Amen."
	PRACTICE the Hebrew of lines 5—7 at least twice.

POINT OUT that this concluding paragraph emphasizes the hope for God's blessings of favor, wisdom and peace. TEACH the tune, line by line.

9. PRACTICE the entire *Birkat ha-Mazon* once more, this time singing. Have everyone chant the entire *Zimmun* section.

ENCOURAGE the participants to practice the *Birkat ha-Mazon* at home.

10. REVIEW the "Practical Questions and Answers" about *Birkat ha-Mazon* in the textbook. ACKNOWLEDGE that it is the longest of the prayers. SUGGEST that they begin with the *Ḥazan et ha-kol* paragraph and add the others as they can.

ASSIGNMENTS

1. Even though this is the final class session, you may need to REVIEW the reciprocal home hospitality visits. If you have arranged to have the participants invite the host families who originally had them to their home, be sure that everyone is clear on the procedures and arrangements.

2. If you have books and resources on Shabbat observance to share, SHOW THEM to the group and TELL the people where they can acquire these materials for further study.

3. STRONGLY ENCOURAGE the participants to continue their Shabbat Seder observance, continually adding to their expression of the Shabbat. CONGRATULATE them on the giant strides they have taken in the course. REMIND them that most change takes place slowly and that it is perfectly appropriate to proceed one step at a time. RECALL that we have learned from the survey of families that everyone's Shabbat experience is different from each other's and that even our own Shabbat Seders may very well vary somewhat week-to-week depending on what we have decided to try, how the family dynamics are at any particular moment, whether we have guests, and any number of other factors. The response each of us is prepared to make to the commitment of "making Shabbes" is the true *art* of Jewish living.

EVALUATION

1. ASK the participants to give you feedback about the course. You will want to know whether the course met their expectations. Ask them about the clarity of the materials and your explanations.

2. OFFER the people the opportunity for "testimonials" about the course. How has the course affected your Shabbat evenings at home? Has the adoption of a Shabbat table ceremony in your home had an impact on your spouse, your children? Has the course made a difference in your own personal Jewish identity? Would you be interested in taking another such course on Jewish observance in the home?

3. SUGGEST that participants recommend the course to their friends and family who may enjoy learning the art of Jewish living.

4. THANK the people for their feedback. Then, THANK them for coming to the course. WISH them well in their future studies and interactions with Jewish living. And, of course, WISH them many, many Shabbatot of shalom.

IMPLEMENTATION GUIDE FOR THE ART OF JEWISH LIVING: THE SHABBAT SEDER

WHAT IS THE ART OF JEWISH LIVING?

The Art of Jewish Living is a series of courses designed to teach adult learners the meanings and skills of Jewish observance in the home. Designed to be taught to laypeople by laypeople, each course focuses on the home observance of a specific Jewish holiday. The goal of this program is to enable the learner competently to perform the home-based blessings and rituals and to knowledgeably fashion a meaningful family observance of the Jewish holidays.

The first course in *The Art of Jewish Living* series is *The Shabbat Seder.* In 6-8 one and a half hour sessions, participants learn how to create a Friday night table ceremony in the home. The course teaches the basic concepts and meanings of the Friday night home rituals and the skills for conducting the traditional Shabbat table observance in Hebrew and English.

The "art" of Jewish living is in knowing the basic competencies of Jewish observance and being able to compose one's own unique representation of it. While this course teaches the basic meanings and skills of the traditional Shabbat Seder, it also recognizes with uncommon honesty the challenges facing those who wish to make Jewish observance a fact of life in their homes. Using an innovative photo-documentary technique, real families who are meeting these challenges successfully are presented in the study material as models for those who are just learning the art of Jewish living.

The Art of Jewish Living: The Shabbat Seder course utilizes a workshop approach, focusing on the mastery of the skills necessary to create a Shabbat table ritual in the home. The materials designed especially for the course are:

LEARNER'S TEXT

The Art of Jewish Living: The Shabbat Seder by Dr. Ron Wolfson is the basic text for the course. Each chapter presents the concepts, objects, blessings and ritual behaviors for the ten steps in the traditional Shabbat Seder. The blessings are presented in a unique linear format, designed to help students learn the meanings of the prayers and how to chant them in Hebrew, whether they can read Hebrew or must depend on transliterations. A detailed description of the procedures involved in performing ritual behaviors is included, along with a section of practical questions and answers about these practices.

A unique aspect of the Learner's Text is the inclusion of a photo-documentary on real families celebrating Shabbat in their homes. Introduced to the reader in the beginning of the text, these families describe in vivid images their own experiences with the Shabbat Seder ritual. Representing families with young children, families with teenagers, empty-nesters and single parents, their stories bring to life the thrill and the challenge of fashioning a Shabbat experience which is personally meaningful to themselves and their families.

The Learner's Text also includes a section on activities for the creative aspects of the Shabbat celebration and a selected bibliography of resources for further study about the Shabbat experience.

TEACHER'S MANUAL AND IMPLEMENTATION GUIDE

A comprehensive *Teacher's Manual for The Art of Jewish Living: The Shabbat Seder* has been written by Dr. Ron Wolfson. It contains session outlines, detailed instructions for teaching the Hebrew blessings and ritual procedures, and teaching tips for the lay instructor. The Implementation Guide presents suggestions for those charged with instituting the course in synagogue adult education programs.

AUDIOTAPES

An audiotape cassette containing the complete Hebrew blessings of the Shabbat Seder is available with the Teacher's Manual and Implementation Guide. The audiotape presents the Hebrew blessings in a slow, deliberate pace which is easy to follow. While traditional tunes are used to chant the blessings, it is possible to have a local Cantor record a new tape with the tunes used in your local congregation.

SHABBAT SEDER BOOKLETS

The complete step-by-step guide to the traditional Shabbat Seder learned in the course is available in booklet form for use at the Shabbat table. Designed for course graduates who want to have multiple copies of the Shabbat Seder for the use of family members and guests, these inexpensive booklets contain the complete Hebrew, transliteration and English translations of the Shabbat Seder blessings and prayers.

PROMOTIONAL MATERIALS

A beautiful full-color poster advertising the *Art of Jewish Living: The Shabbat Seder* course is available. The poster provides space for individual congregations to list the number of sessions in the course, when it is to be offered and the name of a contact person.

Order forms and publicity flyers are also available.

THE METHOD

The Art of Jewish Living: The Shabbat Seder is designed to be taught to laypeople by laypeople. The teaching of Shabbat is mainly accomplished by personal model. The laypeople who will teach this course to their peers have a most unusual opportunity to share part of their own commitment to Jewish life with others.

Qualified laypeople are trained in the teaching of the AJL program by a local professional, Rabbi or educator or at a number of training opportunities which will be offered by the FJMC. A Committee on the Art of Jewish Living Project is created by the local Men's Club chapter to organize the program's implementation in the synagogue educational plans. Courses are scheduled as often as possible for various synagogue member groups: Men's Club, Sisterhood, Adult Education, parents of religious school children, singles, *ḥavurot*, etc. Once a group of lay teachers has been trained, AS MANY CLASSES AS POSSIBLE should be offered. This will be the beginning of a CAMPAIGN to "MAKE SHABBAT" in the HOMES of SYNAGOGUE FAMILIES.

The Federation of Jewish Men's Clubs pioneered the method of laypeople teaching laypeople with the exceptionally successful Hebrew Literacy Campaign. By organizing a number of trained lay teachers who offered the same session of the Hebrew Literacy course at different times of the day during the week, thousands of adults learned enough basic Hebrew to read the Friday night synagogue worship service. The two keys to the phenomenal success of Hebrew Literacy were (1) the availability of a dedicated cadre of lay teachers and (2) the CAMPAIGN aura which surrounded the project.

By training a group of lay teachers who can teach the *Art of Jewish Living: The Shabbat Seder* course at convenient times throughout the week, a major campaign to recruit participants may be launched with the promise of offering a number of opportunities for taking the course. For example, by training 5 lay teachers, classes on the same lesson may be offered 5 different times during the week. Each of the 5 teachers can pick a time to teach over the 6-8 week span of the course. Thus, on two nights per week, two mornings per week and on Sunday morning opposite Sunday School, 5 classes on Shabbat can be in operation.

The advantages to launching this type of campaign as opposed to offering only one class are clear:

1. Each participant can choose the day and time most convenient to his/her schedule.

2. A participant who misses a session can readily make it up by attending another class that week on that same lesson, thus making it much easier to keep up with the material.

3. If a participant wants more practice with a particular part of the Shabbat Seder, he/she can sit in on another class that week.

4. If a participant does not feel comfortable with a particular teacher, options exist to switch gracefully to another class.

5. By having lay people involved in teaching their peers, there is greater outreach and recruitment; it becomes a community effort, feeding on its own momentum.

6. By creating a Shabbat Home Hospitality Program as part of the AJL course, synagogue families will be hosting each other for Shabbat experiences constantly, thus broadening the sharing of Shabbat within the congregational community.

THE ART OF JEWISH LIVING—THE SHABBAT SEDER TIMETABLE

FOUR MONTHS PRIOR TO BEGINNING THE PROGRAM:

1) Organize AJL committees
2) Recruit teachers
3) Set dates for the course
4) Begin initial publicity efforts

TWO MONTHS PRIOR TO BEGINNING THE PROGRAM:

1) Training session for lay teachers
2) Registration materials sent to potential participants

ONE MONTH PRIOR TO BEGINNING THE PROGRAM:

1) Intensive publicity effort
2) Intensive outreach effort, phone campaign, etc.
3) Send registration material to school parents

TWO WEEKS PRIOR TO BEGINNING THE PROGRAM:

1) Registration begins
2) Organize and schedule rooms for classes
3) Contact lay teachers about registration
4) Order textbooks, audiotapes, etc.

ONE WEEK PRIOR TO BEGINNING CAMPAIGN:

1) Phone registrants to remind them of starting date of class
2) Recheck room assignments, coffee set-ups, etc.
3) Phone teachers to check on last minute details

HOW TO BEGIN AN AJL CAMPAIGN

1. BEGIN IMMEDIATELY. A successful campaign needs as much preparation time as possible.

2. The President of the Men's Club of the congregation must be among the prime movers. If you have no Men's Club—start one. In the meantime, the adult education committee and Sisterhood are possible sponsoring organizations.

3. Make the Rabbi your chief consultant and source of inspiration for the AJL project. Work closely with the Rabbi for suggestions and advice. Get the cooperation of the Rabbi to promote the course at services, meetings and in special letters to the congregation-at-large and to the school families.

4. Appoint a Committee on the Art of Jewish living with high-powered congregational members and leaders of the Men's Club, Sisterhood and adult education committees. Invite other highly respected individuals, synagogue board members and a few potential lay teachers of acknowledged ability. Have a parlor meeting in the home of the Rabbi or an influential congregational member. Acquaint them thoroughly with the purpose and materials of the AJL: The Shabbat Seder. Inspire them and persuade them of the necessity of the campaign to get families to make Shabbat at home. Once they are sold on the campaign to teach the congregation how to do a Shabbat Seder, they will be the best salespeople on your team.

5. Begin to brainstorm ideas on the best ways to implement the program locally. Pinpoint the major areas of the activities necessary to launch a successful campaign. Designate a general chairperson as Campaign Coordinator. This should be a person with experience on major UJA or synagogue campaigns. Set deadlines for the execution of tasks.

6. Why the Men's Club as sponsor of the AJL program? The FJMC is sponsoring this project in Conservative congregations on a national scale. With the successful experience of the Hebrew Literacy Campaign behind it, the Federation of Jewish Men's Clubs is a leading force in innovative Jewish adult education. If your local Men's Club mounted a Hebrew Literacy Campaign, you are a step ahead of the game. Identify those who worked on the previous campaign and recruit them as consultants and workers on this new project.

7. Men's Club sponsorship of this project in no way excludes any other group in the congregation. The AJL program may be sponsored by the Men's Club, but it is for for everybody. Every family in the congregation ought to have some kind of Shabbat observance on Friday night in their home. Our goal is to reach everyone we can. To do so, we must enlist the cooperation of every affiliate group in the congregation.

THE TASKS OF THE AJL: THE SHABBAT SEDER COMMITTEE

The success of the AJL: The Shabbat Seder Campaign will depend greatly on the work of your Campaign Coordinator and the people on his/her committee. The following represents a list of major areas of responsibility which will need to be assigned to committee members:

1. Registration

    a) Develop a registration form.

    b) Set dates for registration drive.

c) Recruit top lay leaders in the congregation to take the program or become lay teachers. Publicize this fact to the congregation.

d) Set class rosters for the different time slots of the week.

e) Make sure that class space is blocked for all classes.

f) Arrange classroom set-ups according to the requirements of the course.

g) Check the scheduling of classes against the congregational master calendar to avoid major conflicts.

2. Teacher Recruitment

a) Recruit laypeople who are:
    1) committed to a Shabbat experience in their homes regularly
    2) knowledgeable about the Shabbat Seder and familiar with the Hebrew blessings
    3) enthusiastic about what Shabbat has meant to them and their family
    4) successful communicators with others

b) Look to membership of Men's Club, Sisterhood, and the general congregation for teachers.

c) Recruit as many teachers as you need for the classes planned, plus others who can act as substitute teachers.

d) It does not matter whether the teacher is female or male. However, all teachers must be open and sensitive to the changing roles in today's families.

e) Ask the Rabbi, educational director, Cantor, chairperson of the adult education committee, and other key congregational leaders for leads. Make a list of prospects. Check out the names of prospective teachers with someone high in the synagogue hierarchy to make sure that they are candidates for teaching positions.

f) Recruit potential teachers by personal contact. The Rabbi, committee chairperson, or other committee members should call on prospects in person to ask them to consider teaching this course. Let them feel honored to be asked.

g) When you approach people to volunteer for teaching, you may get three different reactions:

    1) Some will feel greatly honored and will join enthusiastically in the campaign.

    2) Others may be reluctant to teach because they have never done it before. Assure them that training will be provided. Remind them that they will gain great satisfaction in teaching the course.

    3) Some may tell you that they would love to teach because they know all about Shabbat. Tell them that they must participate in the training program in order to understand the approach taken in the program. This course presents the traditional Shabbat Seder, but it also encourages participants to reach decisions about what their Shabbat celebration will look like. There is no one right way to make Shabbat—there are many right ways to make Shabbat.

h) Since you will have more volunteers to teach than classes, be sure to tell the volunteers that some may be only substitutes and some may be assigned classes that fail to materialize. Have these extra teachers to ensure a supply of substitutes for when people get ill or must pull out at the last minute.

i) Share the list of volunteers with the person in charge of registration to help in assigning teachers to classes.

3. Shabbat Home Hospitality

a) Identify a list of families who celebrate a Friday night table ritual who would be willing to host learners and their families in their homes. These families can represent a variety of Shabbat Seder styles of observance, they need not all include every part of the traditional ceremony. The main criterion for inclusion in this part of the program is their commitment and enthusiasm for the Shabbat Seder ritual in their own family. Since this part of the program comes early in the course, you will need to have this list prepared far in advance of the course.

b) Once the dates of the course have been set, identify the first Friday night after the start of classes as AJL Home Hospitality Shabbat. Send a letter to the Home Hospitality Host families asking them to schedule this date and plan on welcoming a family into their home.

c) Inform the Home Hospitality families that they may be invited to the homes of learners sometime after the conclusion of the course. Ask them if their Shabbat observance would allow them to participate in this part of the program. Some Shabbat observant families will not be able to drive to learner's homes for the reciprocal visit. You should know this in advance so the learner is aware that it may be impossible to invite the host family to their home for Shabbat at the end of the course.

d) Prepare a list of Home Hospitality families for the lay teachers so they may match up learners with hosts. The Teacher's Manual contains a section on how to implement this part of the program in the classroom itself.

e) If Home Hospitality is not possible in your congregation, schedule a culminating Shabbat Dinner in the synagogue for the learners and their families at which they may demonstrate what they have learned. Such a Shabbat Dinner in the synagogue, attended by the learners from all the courses and their families, can be a major undertaking in and of itself. Plan accordingly by assigning a member of the committee to coordinate such an event.

4. Publicity

a) Publicity and public relations are at the heart of any campaign. The message to get across is that we are reaching out to every synagogue family to help them learn the art of Jewish living by making Shabbat eve an important time in their home. We want a large turn-out of people. We want it to be exciting for the learners. We have an opportunity to link families in the congregation through the Home Hospitality aspects of this campaign in a unique and meaningful way.

b) Publicity channels include:

1) Every newspaper in the community—Anglo-Jewish, English, metropolitan, suburban, local, free distribution, calendars, etc.
2) Radio and TV
3) Bulletins of the congregation, the Men's Club, Sisterhood, school, youth group, *havurot*, etc.
4) Direct mail to members of the congregation, Men's Club, Sisterhood, school parents, nursery school parents, singles, youth groups, *havurot*, etc.
5) Posters. Order multiple copies of the beautiful full-color publicity poster for the AJL: The Shabbat Seder Project. It has on it place to put the number of sessions in the course, the dates, and who to contact. Put them up on the congregational bulletin boards and on public bulletin boards in the community.
6) Be sure someone on the committee is knowledgeable in public relations and can take on this task. He/She should be able to write a publicity release, a feature story and know how to follow up on contacts in the media. Look for PR types in your congregation to help with these contacts.
7) Story ideas include: the nationwide AJL campaign, endorsements by national and local figures, the schedule of classes, the innovative text materials, the lay teachers, the students, and the Home Hospitality aspect to the program.

5. Budget

a) Estimate the expenses in running the course. You will need to decide if you will produce a publicity flyer to mail to the congregation. The posters may be ordered from the FJMC. Most lay teachers will volunteer their time, but you may decide to offer a token honorarium. If you are planning a culminating Shabbat Dinner, you will need to estimate the costs.

b) Decide on a fee structure for the course. Some congregations will offer the course at no charge. Others will find that charging even a modest fee seems to ensure a better attendance and a more serious attitude among learners. Be sure no one is turned away for lack of funds.

c) The textbooks and audiotapes may be purchased directly from the FJMC or they may be available at a local Jewish bookstore. You should order enough textbooks and supplementary materials to have one for each participant in the course. You will need to decide what to charge participants for these materials.

d) If you are making your own audiotapes of blessings, you must figure your costs and set a charge for the tapes.

TEACHER TRAINING SEMINAR

1. All lay teachers who teach in the *Art of Jewish Living: The Shabbat Seder* Program must participate in a teacher training seminar prior to the start of classes.

2. The seminar may be led by the Rabbi, the Cantor, the educational director, a knowledgeable lay person, a teacher in the school, or an outside expert.

3. The seminar consists of two two hour sessions. One session is a simulation of the Shabbat Seder demonstration; the other is a training session reviewing the materials and outline of the course and tips on teaching adults.

4. The trainer may receive additional suggestions on how to run the teacher training Seminars by writing the FJMC office in New York.

ALTERNATIVE COURSE SCHEDULES

The Teacher's Manual for the *Art of Jewish Living: The Shabbat Seder* course organizes the material into 6 sessions of from 1 and 1/2 to 2 hours each. Our experience is that some congregations will have very specific time frames in which they will want to place this program. Since the material flows from week to week, the schedules can be rather flexible.

A major decision must be made by the Committee on AJL along with the Rabbi. That decision relates to how much you want to teach of the Shabbat Seder in this course. Obviously, the basic parts of the Seder will be taught. However, we have found in our field-testing that some decisions must be made about some of the Hebrew blessings of the lesser known parts of the Seder if time is limited. Areas to consider for teaching in English rather than Hebrew are: the blessings for children, the *Vayekhulu* paragraph introducing the *Kiddush*, a number of *z'mirot*, and some parts of the *Birkat ha-Mazon*.

On the other hand, we anticipate that some congregations will choose to lengthen the course to a maximum number of sessions in order to cover the entire traditional Shabbat Seder, including the complete version of the *Birkat ha-Mazon*.

Rather than leave these decisions up to the individual teacher, the Committee should consider what the objectives are to be in offering this program and offer guidance to the lay teacher on what to include in the course. Much of this decision will depend on available timeframes for teaching the class. Of course, it is always possible to extend the number of sessions if necessary.

The following are three alternative schedules for the AJL: The Shabbat Seder course:

6 SESSIONS—1 and 1/2—2 HOURS EACH

Session 1	Introductions
	Shabbat Seder Demonstration
Session 2	*Hakhanah L'Shabbat*
	Hadlakat Nerot
Session 3	*Shalom Aleikhem*
	Birkot ha-Mishpahah
Session 4	*Kiddush*
Session 5	*Netilat Yadayim*
	Ha-Motzi
	Seudat Shabbat
Session 6	*Z'mirot*
	Birkat ha-Mazon
	Creating Your Own Shabbat Seder

8 SESSIONS—1 and 1/2 HOURS EACH

Session 1	Introductions
	Shabbat Seder Demonstration
Session 2	*Hakhanah L'Shabbat*
	Hadlakat Nerot
Session 3	*Shalom Aleikhem*
	Birkot ha-Mishpahah
Session 4	*Kiddush*
Session 5	*Netilat Yadayim*
	Ha-Motzi
Session 6	*Seudat Shabbat*
	Z'mirot
Session 7	*Birkat ha-Mazon*
Session 8	Creating Your Own Shabbat Seder

10 SESSIONS—1 HOUR EACH

Session 1	Introductions *Shabbat Seder Demonstration*
Session 2	*Hakhanah L'Shabbat* *Hadlakat Nerot*
Session 3	*Shalom Aleikhem*
Session 4	*Birkot ha-Mishpahah*
Session 5	*Kiddush*
Session 6	*Netilat Yadayim* *Ha-Motzi*
Session 7	*Seudat Shabbat* *Z'mirot*
Session 8	*Birkat ha-Mazon I*
Session 9	*Birkat ha-Mazon II or* *Hallah Baking*
Session 10	Creating Your Own Shabbat Seder

The Art of Jewish Living

The Shabbat Seder

Teacher's Guide

by Dr. Ron Wolfson

A Project of

The Federation of Jewish Men's Clubs
and
The University of Judaism

Printed in the USA
CPSIA information can be obtained
at www.ICGtesting.com
JSHW052014140824
68134JS00006B/115

9 781683 362920